The Performer's Anthology

The Performer's Anthology

AN INTERNATIONAL COLLECTION OF DRAMA, PROSE AND POETRY

Compiled and Edited by

Ken Pickering

JANUS PUBLISHING COMPANY
London, England

First published in Great Britain 2008
by Janus Publishing Company Ltd,
105–107 Gloucester Place,
London W1U 6BY

www.januspublishing.co.uk

All introductory material, translations and adaptations
Copyright © 2008 Kenneth Pickering

British Library Cataloguing-in-Publication Data
A catalogue record for this book is available from the British Library

ISBN 978-1-85756–643-7

Cover Design: Kevin Mwangy

Printed and bound in Great Britain
Produced by Digital Book Print Ltd

Recommended for use in auditions, festivals and examinations in speech, drama, communication and theatre arts at all levels.

ACKNOWLEDGEMENTS

The editor thanks and gratefully acknowledges the help of the following in the compilation and production of this anthology:

Madhulika Varma in Mumbai; Amanda Lewis at the Ottawa School of Speech and Drama; John Nicholas at Dramatic Lines; Zita Denholm at Triple D Books; Dr Gillian Bickley in Hong Kong, Annette Kosseris-Haynes at Kindamindi; Tracey Waterman and Richard J. Archer at Xpress Printing; my colleagues Charlotte at IATE and Freni, Olivia and Georgia at Trinity; Claire and Jeannie at Janus and all the authors, publishers and copyright holders listed in the Sources section at the end of this book.

ABOUT THE EDITOR

Professor Ken Pickering is a playwright, librettist, teacher and theatre practitioner who has been the chief examiner for speech and drama at the London College of Music and Trinity/Guildhall and for GCSE Drama. He is currently the chief examiner for performing arts degrees at various leading theatre schools and consultant to Stagecoach Theatre Arts. He has been the visiting professor of theatre at Gonzaga University USA and is a founder director of the Institute for Arts in Therapy and Education in London.

Students and teachers using this anthology will find additional help in the handbook *From Page to Performance*, by Ken Pickering, published by Trinity College, London and distributed by Dramatic Lines.

CONTENTS

INTRODUCTION

Although the pieces contained in this anthology are designed to provide suitable performance material for auditions and for the graded examinations offered by awarding and examining bodies throughout the English-speaking world, their primary purpose is to engage potential performers with a sense of narrative, expressive vocabulary and sheer enjoyment. The sections take their titles from the levels agreed by various awarding bodies in speech and drama in consultation with the Qualifications and Curriculum Authority (QCA) for England and Wales and the similar body for Northern Ireland. FOUNDATIONS offers material for use up to Grade 3, the INTERMEDIATE section is for Grades 4 and 5 and the ADVANCED COLLECTION is intended for Grades 6–8. However, all the pieces might be useful for creative work in schools, colleges and performing arts groups as well as for a wide range of performance situations and opportunities.

The pieces are in no way prescriptive and may be used in a variety of ways. They are arranged in roughly ascending order of length and complexity and include stories, poems and play extracts for use by individuals, pairs or groups. In some cases, a single piece may be used by a group, but may also contain an appropriate passage for use by an individual.

Involvement with pieces from the first section will help to establish the foundations on which future development and success will depend. It is important to make choices that reflect the progressive mastery of the process by which print becomes an engaging performance. There needs to be a sense of ownership and total understanding if we are to avoid what is merely audible print. Teachers are therefore encouraged to help students to select material that is at their natural level of understanding rather than assume that a grade is defined solely by the difficulty of the piece.

I hope that this anthology will form the basis of creative and exciting work and that all the material will be used with the same imagination and enjoyment that lies behind the writing.

Sources of all the pieces contained within this anthology are detailed at the end of the book and you are encouraged to explore these further, particularly when you have used an 'extract'. Where an extract has been taken from an established classic, you will find that there are many published versions available.

FOUNDATIONS

Stories to Read, Tell and Act:

We begin with a collection of stories from all over the world. Some of them are complete and others are parts of longer stories. You can learn them by heart, or tell them in your own words; you can use all or part of them. Some of the stories are written as plays, but you can also make any of the other stories into plays. You can turn the plays into stories for telling or you can use some actions as you tell any of them. Some of these stories and plays can be performed with dance and music and/or for radio or video purposes.

The Lion and the Mouse: a fable by Aesop.
(A tale from ancient Greece circa 600 BC.)

King Lion was dozing in the sunshine near his lair when a tiny mouse, who had lost her way, ran over his nose by mistake and woke him up.

The huge lion was very annoyed and grabbed the frightened little animal with his great paws. He was just about to crush the mouse to pieces, but the mouse began to plead for mercy and told the lion it was all an accident and she hadn't meant to upset him.

'Besides,' said the mouse, 'your Majesty doesn't need to waste time or dirty your paws with a little creature like me!'

The lion was rather amused by the mouse and, smiling down at her, he decided to let her go. She scurried away to safety.

A few days later, the lion was wandering in the forest when he became caught in the ropes of a trap that some hunters had left and, however hard he tried, he could not get free.

Realising that he was trapped, the lion let out a mighty roar that could be heard throughout the entire forest. The little mouse heard it and recognised the voice of the animal who had spared her life.

Very quickly, she ran to where the noise was coming from and, realising what the problem was, began nibbling at the ropes. Soon, the lion was able to wriggle free and escape. He understood that it was the tiny mouse who had saved him.

Both the lion and the mouse had learned that it is always best to be kind and that however small you may be, you can often return a good deed.

Joha and his Ten Donkeys: an Arabic story

(Translated and adapted by Susannah Pickering-Saqqa.)

One day, Joha bought ten donkeys from the market. He felt very pleased with himself and started to drive them towards his home. As he was on his way home, he jumped up and rode on one of the donkeys. After a while, as he was going along the road, he counted the donkeys and found that there were only nine. So he got off the donkey he was riding and counted again. This time, he found that there were ten! So he said to himself, 'That's strange, if I walk I will gain a donkey and if I ride I will lose one!'

Magic Words: an Eskimo legend

In the very early time,

When both people and animals lived on earth,

A person could become an animal if he or she wanted to

And an animal could become a human being.

Sometimes they were people

And sometimes animals

And there was no difference.

All spoke the same language.

That was the time when words were like magic.

The human mind had mysterious powers.

A word spoken by chance

Might have strange consequences.

2

It would suddenly come alive

And what people wanted to happen could happen –

All you had to do was say it.

Nobody could explain this:

That's the way it was.

The Monkey and the Crocodile: a story from *The Panchatantra*.
(A collection of traditional Indian stories.)

One day the crocodile's wife pretended to be very ill. She shed tears as though she was in great pain. The crocodile was sad his wife was ill. He sat by her side and said, 'What can I do to help?'

'I am very ill,' said his wife. 'The doctor said I would get well only if I ate a monkey's heart.'

'A monkey's heart?'

'Yes, a monkey's heart. You must get your friend's heart if you want me to get well.'

'How can I do that? He is my only friend and I cannot think of doing him any harm.'

'Then go and live with your friend. You don't love your wife; you only love your friend. You want to see me dead. Then you can live with him always.'

The crocodile shed more tears. He did not know what to do.

'You don't love me,' said his wife. 'I have decided to end my life. When you come back today you will find me dead.'

The crocodile began to think. As a husband, it was his duty to look after his wife. He decided to save her life.

The Fish of Maui: a Maori legend from Aotearoa, New Zealand

The half-god Maui was fishing one day with his brothers when he landed a giant fish. Maui's brothers did not really want to take him fishing that day because he was known as a trickster and rarely went fishing. But his sisters-in-law had been berating him for his laziness.

Before the expedition, Maui went to the burial cave of his grandmother and stole her jawbone to make a magic hook. Then he hid himself under some mats on board his brothers' canoe. Once they were at sea, he came out of hiding and asked his brothers for some bait for his hook. When they refused, he punched himself in the nose and smeared the blood onto the hook so that he could also fish.

Almost at once he got a bite: a huge bite, pulling the hook and line down deep. Maui heaved and pulled while his brothers paddled the canoe to try to lift the fish from the bottom. When, at last, it came to the surface, the fish was as big as the land.

With the fish lying on the surface, the brothers all started to argue about what to do with it. Maui thought that he should find a priest to bless his wonderful catch and went off in search of one. The brothers, however, were impatient and jumped on the fish, trying to hack at its flesh.

The giant fish wriggled and twisted, and its skin rucked and buckled into mountains, valleys and ravines and, by the time that Maui had returned with the priest, the flesh had turned to soil and rock. The fish was now an island.

The outline of this island still looks like the huge skate that Maui caught and that is why The North Island of New Zealand is called Te Ika a Maui: the fish of Maui.

The Obstinate Hodja: a story from Turkey

(Hodja is the Turkish word for a wise teacher. The folk stories of Nasreddin Hodja are great favourites in Turkey.)

Early one morning, when Nasreddin Hodja and his wife were still fast asleep in bed, their donkey started to bray loudly in his stable. The noise woke Hodja up.

The donkey was braying because he was hungry, and Hodja made up his mind to make his wife get up and feed him.

So he poked his wife, saying, 'Wake up, dear. The donkey is braying because he is hungry. Please get up and feed him.'

His wife, who was only half awake, said, 'Oh no, dear. It's your turn,' and she pulled the bedclothes up over her head.

But, Hodja did not give up. 'Wake up, dear. The poor donkey is hungry, he wants his breakfast. He won't be quiet unless you feed him.'

But Hodja's wife answered, 'Don't be so obstinate, husband, you go and feed the donkey, you know it's your turn!' And she did not lift her head from the pillow.

Hodja said, 'You are quite wrong, my dear, it was me, not you, who fed the donkey yesterday. Come along now, up you get!'

Hodja's wife realised that he was determined to make her feed the donkey, but she was just as determined that she was not going to.

So she sat up in bed beside him and said, very firmly, 'No, no, no! Don't you remember our agreement? We would take it in turns to feed the donkey. I fed him yesterday and it's your turn today!'

Hodja would not budge. 'That can't be true, dear, you are making a mistake.'

But before he could finish speaking, his wife interrupted and said, 'No, it's you who is wrong. Now don't be so obstinate. Go and feed the poor animal!'

It was no use though. Hodja had made up his mind that whatever it took, he would make his wife feed the donkey, and he started to think about how he could get his own way.

He turned to his wife with a broad smile on his face and said, 'My dear, I think I have the answer to our problem. As soon as I have finished my explanation, the first person to say anything will have to feed the donkey. Is that agreed?'

'OK, I agree,' his wife said reluctantly, and, pressing her lips firmly together, she sat very still and upright beside her husband.

For the next two hours, neither of them said anything.

Now, you should understand that Hodja's wife loved to chatter and gossip and she was bursting to say something. She knew that she would lose if she stayed there. So she slipped out of bed and went quietly out of the room and went to visit her next-door neighbours. And there she sat, talking excitedly, while Hodja stayed in his bed as still as a stone.

I expect you know that people from the village would often call on Hodja to ask his help and advice and this day was like any other. But this day, even though people crowded round his bed, Hodja would neither speak nor answer their questions.

The villagers tried to think of a way to make Hodja start talking and before long, they started to carry away his furniture: first the chairs, then the wardrobe and then everything else in the bedroom. Of course, Hodja could not say anything or he would lose his bet with his wife.

Finally, in desperation, the neighbours even took Hodja's nightcap from his head. And he said not one word.

Around noon, Hodja's wife sent the neighbour's daughter with a bowl of soup and these instructions: 'If he says anything to you, you must repeat it to me.'

The girl went into Hodja's room and asked where she should put the soup. Hodja pointed to every part of the room and then to his bare head: trying to explain what had happened. But, from Hodja's miming, the girl thought he meant: 'Walk round the room and then come and pour the soup on my head!'

So that was what she did. And Hodja stayed silent.

The girl was frightened when she saw Hodja sitting so still and silent and she ran back home.

Hodja's wife was waiting anxiously and asked the girl what had happened. When the girl told her she was horrified and she screamed, 'O my goodness, you have scalded my husband!' She ran home as fast as she could.

Hodja was still sitting up in bed with soup all over his head and face and it was even dripping off the end of his nose. His wife tried to wipe him clean, saying, 'I'm so sorry for what that silly girl did!'

A satisfied smile spread across Hodja's face. 'Go and feed the donkey,' he said, 'you have lost the contest!'

Loreley and the Sailor: a saga of Father Rhine

(The River Rhine is the main and most important river in Germany. There are places where the river is dangerous for navigation and mists often swirl around. Many legends have grown up: the Loreley is one of the most famous and is the subject of a well-known song.)

There has always been a lot of singing on my banks and the most beautiful singing comes from my daughter, the water nymph, Loreley. She looks and sounds so wonderful that nobody can resist her. Her favourite spot on the river is a steep rock near a bend where there are whirlpools and high cliffs. Sailors have to be very careful at this point, because the navigation is so difficult and dangerous.

Once, a young captain was steering his boat through this narrow part of the river and he heard Loreley singing. He was so enraptured that he looked up to see where the enchanting sound was coming from and he saw Loreley sitting high on a rock with her long hair tumbling down towards him. He was so transfixed that he could not take his eyes from her and his boat went spinning towards the rocks and was smashed to pieces.

That rock is now named after my daughter, but she did not always sit there. Some years later, a monk named Goar, who loved fishing, went to sit at that spot on the river with his rod and line. When Loreley saw him coming, she started to sing and did everything possible to attract his attention. Goar, however, took no notice of her and told her to move away so that he could concentrate on his fishing. Loreley was so ashamed and humiliated that she fled and Goar felt so much inner strength now that he had resisted her that he became known as St Goar. There is a town named after him just opposite the Loreley rock even today.

Little Red Riding Hood: a fairy story from France

(Charles Perrault, who lived from 1628 to 1703, was the first person to write this story down. When the Grimm brothers included it in their collection more than 100 years later, they gave the story a happy ending; you might like to do the same!)

There was once a little girl and her mother loved her very much. Her grandmother was also very fond of her and had made a little red hood for her that suited her so well that everyone called her "Little Red Riding Hood".

One day, her mother baked some cakes and said to her: 'Go and see how your grandmother is, because I hear that she is ill. Take her a cake and this small pot of butter.'

Little Red Riding Hood set off at once. Her grandmother lived in another village on the far side of the wood and, as she was going through the wood, she met Master Wolf. The wolf wanted to eat her but did not dare, because some woodcutters were working nearby; so he asked her where she was going.

The little girl did not know that it was dangerous to stop and talk to a wolf, so she said: 'I am going to see my grandmother.'

'Does she live far from here?' asked the wolf.

'Oh yes,' said Little Red Riding Hood, 'it's beyond that mill you can see over there, in the first house in the village.'

'I see,' said the wolf, and ran off at top speed.

Little Red Riding Hood took a longer route and stopped along the way to gather flowers and nuts and chase butterflies.

The wolf soon reached the grandmother's house and knocked: rat-a-tat.

'Who's there?'

'It's your granddaughter, Little Red Riding Hood,' said the wolf, imitating her voice. 'I've brought you a cake and a pot of butter from my mother.'

The grandmother, who was not feeling very well and was lying in bed, called out: 'Pull the catch and you will loose the latch.'

The wolf pulled the catch and the door opened. He sprang on the old lady and ate her all up, because he had had nothing to eat for three days. Then he shut the door and got into the bed to wait for Little Red Riding Hood.

Presently, she arrived and knocked at the door: rat-a-tat.

'Who's there?'

At first, Little Red Riding Hood was afraid when she heard the wolf's gruff voice, but then she thought her grandmother must have a cold, so she answered: 'It's your granddaughter, Little Red Riding Hood. I have brought you a cake and a pot of butter from my mother.'

Making his voice a little less gruff, the wolf said: 'Pull the catch and you'll loose the latch.'

Little Red Riding Hood pulled the catch and the door opened.

The wolf hid himself under the bedclothes and said: 'Put the cake and the little pot of butter on the bread bin and climb into bed with me.'

Little Red Riding Hood did so and was very surprised to see how her grandmother looked in her nightclothes. She said to her: 'What big arms you have, Grandmother!'

'All the better to hug you with, my dear!'

'What big legs you have, Grandmother!'

'The better to run with, my child!'

'What big ears you have, Grandmother!'

'The better to hear you with, my child!'

'What big eyes you have, Grandmother!'

'The better to see you with, my child!'

'What big teeth you have, Grandmother!'

'They're to eat you with!'

And so saying, the wicked wolf sprang on Little Red Riding Hood and ate her up.

This story teaches that the very young,
Should never trust a stranger's artful tongue.

Extract from *Toytown* by S. G. Hulme Beaman

Early the next morning, the Mayor of Toytown was seated in his study at the town hall. He was feeling very annoyed and irritated, for he had been taken away from his breakfast before he had half finished and had only had time for one slice of marmalade. This was due to the fact that Mr Growser had called, demanding to see the Mayor on most important business; and now the two gentlemen sat opposite each other while Mr Growser was explaining why he had called.

'It's disgraceful!' Mr Growser was saying. 'Disgraceful! It ought not to be allowed. It wouldn't be allowed in any decent town. Where are the police? What are the police doing to allow such things to happen?'

'I don't know yet what has happened,' replied the Mayor. 'I must ask you to kindly explain, and not to shout so. Also, kindly refrain from thumping your umbrella on my new carpet.'

'I shall thump my umbrella wherever I like and as hard as I like!' cried the old gentleman. 'It's only me that keeps this town awake. And now I have had one of my windows broken! Scandalous! Disgraceful!'

'Yes, but what has happened?' the Mayor asked.

'Don't I keep on telling you!' Mr Growser cried. 'My window has been broken; my window! W – I – N – D – O – window! Someone has thrown a stone through it!'

The Mayor rose from his chair and stared at Mr Growser with great dignity. 'And did you tear me away from my breakfast just to tell me that one of your windows has been broken?' he asked.

'No, sir, I did not!' replied Mr Growser. 'I also desired to tell you that you ought to be ashamed to call yourself Mayor of a town where such things are allowed. I say what I think, sir. I say what I think. Breakfast indeed! You sit there gorging yourself with bread and treacle while the whole town is going to rack and ruin.'

'I'm afraid that the matter of broken windows is hardly my department, Mr Growser,' said the Mayor. 'You should apply to the police. That is what the police are for.'

'Oh, indeed, Mr Mayor! Indeed! I'm glad to know that; I have often wondered what the police were for. And now I do know I have no hesitation in saying that the police ought to be thoroughly ashamed of themselves!'

The Mayor was just about to utter a stern reply to this when his secretary came bustling in.

'Your worship,' said the secretary, 'two animals have arrived with some very curious news. It concerns the constable. You must have noticed he did not appear here this morning as usual; the animals in question seem to be in a rather excited state. They say they know why he is absent.'

'I know why he is absent!' cried Mr Growser. 'He's ashamed to show his face. And no wonder!'

The Mayor ignored the old gentleman and ordered his secretary to admit the callers; and in a few moments, Larry and Dennis stepped into the room. The lamb was carrying the policeman's helmet, and both animals looked very muddy and untidy.

'Oh, sir, oh, Mr Mayor, sir!' began Larry.

'What is it, my lamb? What is it?' asked the Mayor. 'Take your time, my good animal, take your time.'

'Oh, sir, oh, sir, we've come to tell you about Mr Ernest,' cried Larry.

'Ernest the constable that was,' Dennis added.

'That was!' cried the Mayor. 'Isn't he still the constable?'

Dennis shook his head sadly and Larry rubbed his eyes with a very muddy little hoof.

'He's been stolen by the fairies,' said Larry.

'Stolen by what?' cried the Mayor.

'The fairies, Mr Mayor, sir.'

'From under our very noses, stolen,' Dennis added.

'Stuff and nonsense!' shouted Mr Growser. 'Fairies indeed! Whoever heard of such a thing? He's afraid to face me, that's what it is. He's hiding. He's ashamed!'

'I feel sure you must be mistaken, my good animals,' remarked the Mayor. 'Quite apart from the fact that there is – ahem – some doubt as to whether there are – in short – such things as fairies, I certainly feel that it would take quite a lot of fairies to steal a large, able-bodied policemen. Did you actually witness the – ahem – kidnapping?'

Extract from *Snow White and the Seven Dwarfs*
(A play by Ken Pickering.)

In the Forest the gloomy light gradually reveals a small cottage with tiny furniture and a table showing the remains of a meal. It is all rather untidy.

Enter SNOW WHITE, *as if she is still following the nymphs in a dream. She stops and gazes at the cottage.*

SNOW WHITE What is this? Who can live in this dear little house? It's so tiny, so cute ... this little door ... I can't believe it ... I wonder if there's anyone at home. 'Hello! Hello! ... Is there anyone there?' Doesn't seem to be! I wonder where they are! Perhaps I could try the door ... it's not locked [*opens the door and enters cautiously*]. They must be very trusting people. [*Calling*] 'Excuse me ... is there anybody there?' Strange, they obviously went out in a great hurry ... it's rather untidy ... I would never be allowed to leave my room this untidy! I just wonder who they can be. The chairs are too small for me ... well, perhaps this one is a bit better [*sits in it*]. Some of these people must be so tiny ... I think I'll sit on this stool ... it's much more comfortable [*she does so*]. I'm hungry ... I must eat something ... it looks as though they have been preparing a meal ... or have just finished one ... I can't tell ... there must be a clean plate somewhere ... ah here's one ... and some bread and vegetables ... now where's a knife and fork ... [*starting to eat*] mmm ... I'm absolutely starving. I'm sure they won't mind sharing the food with me! I'll explain when they come back ... whoever they are ... I must drink something ... all that running in the forest has made me so thirsty [*she takes a cup and pours herself a drink*]. That's better. [*She gets up from the table*] There must be quite a lot of these little people living here. [*Counting the chairs and stools*] One ... two ... three ... four ... five ... six ... seven! Seven small people in one small house ... they are not all quite the same size ... look at these beds ... they make me feel sleepy just looking at them ... perhaps I could try one. [*She lies on one of the bed*] ... Oh that's too short ... there's no room for my legs ... let me try this one. [*She moves to another bed*] Oh, that's much too hard ... there must be a better one. [*She moves and feels another bed with her hands*] ... Ah, this one feels good [*she lies on it*]. It is good ... mmm ... it's so comfortable here. I must just have a sleep ... then I must try to find my way home [*as if in a dream*]. Oh no. I can't really go home. The wicked queen will try to kill me ... I don't know where I can go ... but I don't really care now ... I'm so sleeeeeepy [*yawning and settling down to sleep*].

> [*The stage grows dark and then we hear the sounds of the* SEVEN DWARFS *approaching, singing a work song as they return from a day in the mines*

Extract from *Alice in Wonderland* by Lewis Carroll

(You can use this for solo speeches or as a scene for two.)

A grassy bank. ALICE *is curled up with a book*

ALICE [*sleepily*]. Stupid book! No pictures – no conversations ... [*throws it down*]. What shall I do? Make a daisy chain? Then I shall have to get up and pick daisies. [*Yawns*] O-h-h-h! I'm so sleepy – so sleepy.

> [*Drops her head on her arm and lies for a minute as if she were really asleep*

Enter the WHITE RABBIT.

> [ALICE *raises her head and looks at him drowsily. Then, as he takes a watch from his waistcoat pocket, she stares at him with suddenly awakened interest. He scutters away, not noticing an envelope which he pulled out of his pocket with the watch, and which has fallen to the ground*

ALICE [*staring after him*] Rabbits haven't waistcoat pockets! At least, I didn't know they had! Rabbits haven't watches in their waistcoat pockets!

Re-enter WHITE RABBIT, muttering to himself and looking about.

RABBIT The Duchess! The Duchess! Oh my dear paws! Oh my fur and whiskers! What'll she say if she doesn't get the Queen's invitation! She'll get me executed, as sure as ferrets are ferrets! Where can I have dropped it, I wonder!

ALICE If you please, sir, it is just where you are looking – [*The RABBIT whisks round, stares at Alice in terror, and darts away*]. Silly little thing! [*She gets up and crosses to where the letter lies.*] There it is, sure enough! [*Picks it up*] And what is this? [*Picks up a little bottle with a big label on it. Reads label.*] Drink me! [*Looking at it cautiously*] I wonder if it's poison. [*Takes out cork and sniffs it*] It smells very good! [*Tastes it*] It tastes very nice! Like cherry tart and custard – [*Tastes again*] – like cherry tart and custard and pineapple and roast turkey and toffee and hot buttered toast. [*Drinks it*] Oh, I've finished it all off! What a curious feeling! I seem to be shutting up like a telescope! [*Looks at letter*] "For the Duchess. An invitation from the Queen to play croquet." I wonder where the Duchess lives. [*Looking round*] Why, there's a little door! I never saw that little door before!

Further extract from *Alice in Wonderland*

(Adapted for stage by Evelyn Smith.)

The DUCHESS has just thrown her baby to ALICE. ALICE arranges the baby in a comfortable position.

ALICE Don't move your arms and legs about like that, in all directions – just like a starfish. [*Thoughtfully*] If I don't take this child away with me they're sure to kill it in a day or two. Wouldn't it be murder to leave it behind? [*The BABY grunts*] [*Sharply*] Don't grunt. That's not at all a proper way of expressing yourself.

[*BABY grunts again. ALICE pulls back the veil from its face and looks at it very anxiously*] You have a very turned-up nose, my dear! It's more like a snout than a real nose! Your eyes are extremely small for a baby ... I don't like the look of this thing at all. [*The CAT laughs. ALICE looks at it, and again looks at the BABY*] If you are going to turn into a pig, my dear, I'll have nothing more to do with you. Mind now! [*BABY grunts so violently that Alice jumps and looks at it in horror*] It is a pig! [*Goes quickly to side and puts it out. Stands for a minute looking after it.*] If it had grown up, it would have made a dreadfully ugly child, but it makes rather a handsome pig, I think ... Lots of babies would do very well as pigs, if only one knew the right way to change them ... [*Turns to CAT*]. Cheshire Puss – [*CAT grins*] – would you tell me, please, which way I ought to go from here?

The next extract is a speech from the beginning of a play. You may wish to use it as a solo piece or to develop into longer scenes.

Stories, plays and poems quite often begin or end with a dream: here is a good example and you might like to continue the story or speech in your own words.

Extract from *The Parlement of Foules*
(Adapted from Geoffrey Chaucer)

A Garden

> [*At the front of the stage, the DREAMER lies curled up, with his head on a pile of books. He half rises, propping himself on one arm, and speaks to the audience*

DREAMER This morning I found an old book, written in old writing, and I liked it so much that I read and read all day. Then night came, when all the little beasts stop working and playing and, because there was no light, I had to stop reading and get ready for bed. When the weary hunter sleeps, he dreams of the woods; the judge of the cases he tries; the carter of how his carts rattle along; the rich man of gold. The knight dreams of fighting with his foe, and the lover of his lady. And so it is quite natural that I should dream of the man in the book I had been reading and reading and reading all day. He came and stood by my bed and said he was very glad I loved the old, torn book so much, and that he would like to give me a reward. So he took my hand and brought me to this garden, with a green stone wall round it. It is always spring in this garden. Some of the boughs are green with fresh little leaves; some are all blossomy. There are white, blue, yellow and red flowers growing in the grass, and a river, and cold running streams where swim small fish, silver, with red fins. Wee beasts, rabbits and squirrels, play about. [*Drowsily*] The birds sing, and the wind makes a soft noise in the green leaves – [*More and more drowsily*] The birds – sing – and the wind – together – this is – my dream about – the birds.

> [*Drops back on his book-pillow with his cheek on his hand, and sleeps*

The Panchatantra is a traditional Indian collection of stories for children, usually with animals as protagonists. Kamala Ramchandani-Naharwar has taken five of the stories and written a musical play around them. This excerpt is from the play:

Extract from *The Panchatantra*
by Kamala Ramchandani-Naharwar

A Forest

RABBIT enters

RABBIT Tsk tsk tsk. IIIII … am a rabbit! [*Bows*] The hero of the forest. [*Taps foot*] For I have defeated kings. [*Sings*] Lion Kings! Shall I tell you how? Just watch! I shall hoppit for now. There's a lion around, my dear man, and he may eat you up … [*We hear LIONS roar*] RUNNNNNNN!

LION ROOAAAR! I WANT MY LUNCH! I WANT MY DINNER! Where are the animals! I will eat you up. ROOAAAAR!

RABBIT enters

RABBIT 'OooOOoOoo', 'AaAaAa', 'EeEeeEee'.

LION [*shades his eyes, looks into the audience*] Who's there? It's dark and I can't see!

RABBIT Squeek, squeek! … It's me … One of the animals … Of the forest … Oh King! Your Highness! Sirrrr!

LION [*to AUDIENCE, but pointing backwards*] All delicious meals out theeeree! [*To RABBIT*] What do you want? Tell me QUICK! Or I shall eat you AAALL!

RABBIT We'll send you … A good dinner … One of us … Will come every day … You won't have to hunt! We'll BE your dinner!

LION I want my LUNCH! ROARRR!

[*BOTH go off*

RABBIT enters

RABBIT Oh dear, oh dear, it's my turn to be eaten by the lion today! Oh dear, oh dear! … I know! [Snaps fingers] I'll FOOL HIM! How clever of me!

[*Hops to one side*

LION enters

LION I want my lunch and dinner, I'm getting thinner and thinner. As you can see, my clothes don't fit me. I just live on plain tea. I'm really getting no dinner as you can plainly see. Roarr.

[*RABBIT comes forward*

RABBIT Hop-hop-hop! Stop-stop-stop! I'm here!

LION ROARRRR! [*Bending over RABBIT*] Just one tiny rabbit for my dinner?

RABBIT [*taps LION on shoulder*] I want to tell you something!

LION YEEEEEES?

RABBIT There were three of us!

> [*Holds up three fingers*

LION YEEEES?

RABBIT But another lion ate the other two ...

LION WHATTT-T-T?!!! ROARRR!

RABBIT ... and he sent me to tell youuuu that HEEEEE is the king of the forest, not YOUUUUUU!

> [*Points finger at LION*

LION [Getting worked up as he listens. Then] ROARRRRRRR! Take me to that other lion ...

RABBIT [*cunningly*] But he is younger ... and stronger ...

LION TAKE MEEEEEEE!!!!

RABBIT Follow me, Your Highness!

> [*BOTH exit*

Re-enter, the LION is bent, holding his back, and using a stick.
We see a WELL half showing

LION Such a long journey [*in a quivery voice*]. My back aches, my knees shake and I'm using a stick! Where is that other lion?

RABBIT Hop-hop-hop! Stop-stop-stop! In his well, sir!

> [*Points to well.*
> *LION wobbles over and peers in*

LION I can see him!

ROOAAR!

> [*ECHO: Rooaar*

I can hear him! ROOAAR!

> [*ECHO: Rooaar*

The action of the musical play *Advent Journey*, by Ken Pickering and Denny Smith, takes place on a journey to Christmas. Three characters: the Seeker, the Wanderer and the Traveller are told by a mysterious voice that they must follow a route along which they must open the windows of an Advent Calendar and be joined by the characters who leap out from those windows. Here is a scene where some of the characters (who move and make sounds to fit their names) are approaching an important part of their journey.

Extract from *Advent Journey*

BALL [*bouncing up to the next window*] Look, here's the next window. Can you remember who's in here?

FLUTE I know ...

TOP Who is it then?

DRUM Listen. Listen.

> [*There are sounds of enormous yawns from inside the window*

BALL, DRUM, FLUTE, TOP [*together*] It's Pudding. The lazy pudding.

> [*TRAVELLER and SEEKER open the window and
> the PUDDING staggers out, stretching and yawning*

PUDDING What's all the fuss about? Can't a Christmas pudding have a bit of rest?

TOP We need you to come with us. You should understand what Christmas is really about ... [*quick spin*]. And we are going on a journey to find the Christmas light ...

PUDDING [*sighing*] I certainly know about Christmas lights. They often set fire to me at Christmas ... singe my top. And they love every minute of it, too. Ooooing and aaaaaaaring at my expense.

TRAVELLER [*horrified*] Who does that?

PUDDING Humans. They can be very cruel you know. Sometimes, they stuff coins in me, too! Right here, in my midriff!

> [*Sighing*

TRAVELLER We promise we don't do anything like that ...

WANDERER Do come along ... Come along and help us on our journey, Pudding. Who is your next-door neighbour? Can you ask them to come too, please?

PUDDING Oh, she'll come all right ... any excuse to dance around and look glamorous!

> [*Knocking on the next window*

PUDDING [*cont.*] Hey, Tinsel, can you stop looking at yourself in the mirror for a moment and come to the window?

TINSEL [*from inside*] Just putting my make-up on, darling. Coming! [*FAIRY TINSEL makes a grand entrance*] Oh, hello. What's this, an expedition?

TOP Yes. We're going on a journey to Christmas and we want you to come too.

19

TINSEL Well, as long as you don't expect me to perch on top of a Christmas tree. It gets very uncomfortable, I'll have you know. Stuck up there for hours on end, prickles all round my legs. Ugh!

DRUM We can't promise; but I'm sure that Flute will play a good tune for you to dance along the way.

TINSEL OOOH, lovely!   [*Already starts dancing*

FLUTE Before I can play your tune we have to help open the other windows ... and you-know-who's in the next one.

SEEKER, WANDERER, TRAVELLER You know who?

BALL, DRUM, FLUTE, TOP PUDDING [*ALL shout together*] Ellibore the Donkey!!

The book and music for this entire play, together with an accompaniment CD can be obtained from Dramatic Lines. (See SOURCES section at the end of this book).

Veronica Bennetts is a leading figure in contemporary performing arts education and has made a number of very successful musical theatre adaptations for young people. In the following extracts, we are introduced to two of the enchanting children's stories by Oscar Wilde. They are published under the collective title of:

Introducing Oscar:

Extract from *The Selfish Giant*

SAM I love this place! Do you know? I only have to put a toe inside the garden and I feel so happy I have to laugh out loud!

[*There is spontaneous general agreement*

AMY It's seven years since the Giant was here. I know it's his garden, but he can't be coming back after all this time, can he?

SUSAN I hope not. But we'd better make the most of it while we've got it.

SAM After all, this garden's our playground ...

GEORGE Our parkland ...

SUSAN Our *Paradise*!

[*The CHILDREN all sing with great joy*

This is Our Playground!   [*Song and dance*

   This is our playground, this is our parkland,

      This is our Paradise.

      No more spelling and no more sums;

      We're outside and we feel the sun.

      This is our playground, this is our parkland,

      This is our Paradise!

[*The CHILDREN all dance joyfully*

   In our garden flowers bloom brightly,

      Leaves whisper softly of better days.

      There are no corridors and no high grey walls

      And no blackboards and no canes.

      This garden's our window

      That brightens today.

      It brings us the sunshine,

      We hope we can stay.

      We so want to stay,

      Oh please say we may!

[*They dance again*

SUSAN [*after a brief pause at end of dance*]   Now, what shall we play?
    How about a game of Tag?

SAM We played that yesterday.

HARRY I know! Let's play Giant's Footsteps.

SUSAN [*shivering*] Ugh, no! That's a bit too much like the real things.
    When-is-a-game-not-a-game?!

TOM What about Blind Man's Buff?   [*ALL agree*

TOM [*cont.*] Here's my tie. Come on, Sue. Ready for the blindfold?

SUSAN No, not me! I hate the dark. Pick someone else.

GEORGE Being scared of the dark is for babies.

SUSAN Then I'll stay a baby!
AMY Blindfold me! I'm not afraid.

> [*AMY is blindfolded and the game begins.
> The other* CHILDREN *easily dodge out of her
> way as* AMY *flounders around*

> *Enter* GIANT

> [*The* CHILDREN *shrink back as the* GIANT
> *appears, watching in silent horror, as* AMY *is
> about to feel her way into his path. The* GIANT
> *grabs her and the* CHILDREN *hide, cowering in
> a tight group, as* AMY *is caught*

GIANT Got you! You little tyke! What are you doing in here?
AMY [*squirming*] Oh please, sir, please! Let me go! We've only been playing.
GIANT PLAYING!!! My own garden is my own garden. Anyone can understand that, and no one is allowed to play in it but me!
AMY [*plucking up courage*] Well then, if that's the case, I think you're a very selfish giant! [*Realising*] Oh please, please, don't hurt me, I didn't mean it ...

> [*Pulling free, running away and hiding
> with the other* CHILDREN

GIANT How on earth did those nuisances get inside in the first place? [*He inspects the imaginary wall downstage and finds the hole*] Now, I can see. What I need is a new wall, a high wall, a thick wall. A wall with no holes in it. I must get building straight away. No one is allowed to play in my garden. Oh no!
CHILDREN [*whispering to the audience without moving*] He was a very selfish giant.

> [*The* CHILDREN *are like statues made of
> stone. They are carried off by the* GIANT *and
> used to make a human wall downstage. The
> GIANT talks to himself as he builds the wall,
> complaining about the children ad-lib finally
> ending with ...*

GIANT ... That should do it. Now, where's that notice? [*He fetches the notice and stands it up*] That should teach them a thing or two, if they can read. They never get taught proper in schools nowadays, especially when it comes to grammaticals. [*Proudly viewing his handy work*] Yes ... just the job! 'Trespassers will be prosecutED'.

[*GIANT exits muttering. The human wall sings*

Extract from *The Happy Prince*

	Dancing in the Darkness	*[Song and dance*
ALL	We're so hungry and we're thirsty,	
	We are very, very cold	
LAVENDER	He is coughing ...	
SHOESHINE	She's been crying.	
PAPER	And her flowers ain't sold.	
SHOESHINE	I am tired ...	
PAPER	And I always cough.	
VI	And I want my mum.	
MATCHIE	And my dad will beat me and give me	
	Strap marks on my bum.	
ALL [*chorus*]	Jigsaw land of poverty,	
	Frozen land of sorrow.	
	All your jigsaw children here	
	Are hiding in your city.	
	The secret of the city.	*[whispered*
	Dancing in the darkness,	*[chorus divides*
	Singing through the pain,	
	Leaping into loneliness,	
	There and back again.	
	There and back again.	
ALL [*chorus*]	Jigsaw land of poverty, etc.	

> [*EVERYONE joins in a dance which expresses their plight and their courage. At the end of the dance they all freeze with the little match-girl holding out her hands and gazing upwards forlornly*

SWALLOW [*shivering*] It's getting very cold. Time I was off to Egypt. Thank you for letting me stay, Your Majesty. I have loved sleeping in my golden bedroom!

PRINCE Swallow, little Swallow, will you stay with me one night longer?

SWALLOW Prince, it's winter, and the chill snow will soon be here. In Egypt, the sun is warm on still blue waters and the palm trees are swaying in the gentle breeze. If I stay here, my wings will freeze. Egypt's calling me, you know. [*Pause*] Next spring, I'll bring you back a beautiful jewel for your swords.

PRINCE Little swallow, I have been watching a little match-girl in the square below. Her matches have fallen in the gutter, they're all spoiled, and her father is going to beat her. Little Swallow, there are other children suffering, too. Will you help me just once more? Please take one of the sapphires and give it to the children.

SWALLOW Please don't ask me to do that. You can't lose one of your beautiful eyes. You're making me cry.

PRINCE Please, do as I command.

> [*The SWALLOW reaches up and plucks an imaginary sapphire from the eye of the HAPPY PRINCE. She swoops down to the children and places the jewel in the little match-girl's upturned hands. TO WIND CHIMES IMPROVISED MUSIC ad-lib as before. The SWALLOW waits a little way away from the group and watches the CHILDREN quizzically. MATCHIE unfreezes. She looks down at her hands and sees the sapphire. She shrieks with delight. Her cries rouse the others*

MATCHIE Hey! Hey! Come and look at this! I don't know where it came from. Look! ... A jewel! Must be worth a small fortune.

[*ALL crowd round and chatter excitedly and shout out a variety of exclamations ad-lib.* PAPER *takes the sapphire from* MATCHIE *and handles it with great curiosity*

PAPER Luvley blue colour, but it's just a bit of glass, Matchie. Nothing special. Don't you raise yer hopes.

SHOESHINE Fall from the sky, did it?

VI Where did it come from, Matchie? How'd it land in yer 'and like that?

MATCHIE I don't know. There was I … just sort of thinking 'bout the dam matches and me dad … and next thing I knew it was just there, all cool in me hands.

SHOESHINE Let me take a look. [*He holds it up to the light and peers closely at it.*] Ooh-er! I'm not so sure this is just any old bit of blue glass, Paper. Look! If I move it round the light sort of cuts right through with bright, sparkly lines.

[*ALL gaze open mouthed as he twists it in the light*

LAVENDER [*slowly, but with excitement and awe*] That's no glass. That's a precious stone, that is.

VI That makes it a sapphire!

MATCHIE Is that like a diamond?

SHOESHINE Just like a diamond! [*They all twirl around, cheering.*] I feel all sort of 'singey' inside. Like I'm full of music.

LAVENDER Yeah, and I've gone all 'dancey' in me tummy.

PAPER Your luck's changing, Matchie.

MATCHIE Oh no, Paper, our luck's changin'. This … um … saff …

VI Sapphire, Matchie. This 'ere sapphire …

MATCHIE This 'ere sapphire belongs to all of us. [*Pointing out friends*] To you, Vi, and her. [*Lavender looks surprised*] Yes, you, Lavender, and you, Paper, and 'specially you, Shoeshine. T'ain't just mine. It's a present to all of us from somebody very kind.

PAPER I don't 'arf feel a song and dance comin' on!

SWALLOW [*to AUDIENCE, innocently*] And I don't 'arf as well!

[*They sing joyfully as the swallow weaves in and out between them*

25

No. 15. Feel the Music of Life!

MATCHIE [*chorus*]   Feel the music of life in the beat of your heart.

FRIENDS   Feel the music of life in the beat of your heart.

MATCHIE   Sense the music of life in the depth of your soul.

FRIENDS   Sense the music of life in the depth of your soul.

MATCHIE   Spinning and whirling like planets and new stars,

FRIENDS   Spinning and whirling like planets and new stars,

MATCHIE   Throbbing and pulsing like rhythms of ole earth.

FRIENDS   Throbbing and pulsing like rhythms of ole earth.

MATCHIE   Feel the music of life in the beat of your heart.

FRIENDS   Feel the music of life in the beat of your heart.

ALL   Binding up the wounds of living,
        Cradling the broken-hearted.
        Touching, lifting spirits crushed,
        Changing sorrow to joy.

[*Chorus*]   Feel the music of life in the beat of your heart. [*Etc*

ALL   Joining in the hoping, longing,
        Mirroring the laughing, crying, carolling
        In rich and poor.
        Changing darkness to light.

The music for this and the previous extract is available from Dramatic Lines. (See SOURCES section at the end of this book.)

Poems to Read, Learn and Perform:

Poems help us to enjoy and understand our world and the people within it; but we can also enjoy the poems *themselves*, because of their interesting words, rhythms and ideas.

We can read a poem quietly to ourselves but, once we speak it aloud, we are 'performing' the poem and we have to find the best way to share the wonderful sounds and ideas that we have discovered.

All the poems in this section are suitable for performing: many of them are written by living writers and these writers come from many different countries. Before you can present your poem to somebody else, you will need to understand every word and be able to explain what it is about and why you have chosen it. You will also need to discover the most effective way to help your listener to enjoy it, too. Some of the poems are written by very young people and you may like to use the space at the end of this anthology to write your own poems.

Hamburgers by Colin Thiele (Australia)

Hamburgers big and Hamburgers small,
Hamburgers pictured and hung on the wall,
Hamburgers jolly and round and fat,
Hamburgers domed like a bowler hat,
Hamburgers served with onion and cheese,
Hamburgers trying their hardest to please,
Hamburgers saucy and Hamburgers plain,
Hamburgers hearty in sunshine or rain,
Hamburgers plump and Hamburgers tall,
The people of Hamburg are Hamburgers all.

Getting Out of Getting Into Bed by Sheree Fitch (Canada)

I'll never understand
Why day turns into night
And I have to go to sleep
And there isn't any light.

Can I have a drink of water?
Then I'll go to bed
My throat is dry without a drink
I'm sure I'll wake up dead.

How about a cracker?
Then I'll go to bed
Better yet, I think I want
A granola bar instead.

Now I have to piddle
Before I go to bed
Well, I wouldn't want a puddle
In the middle of my bed!

To tell the truth
I'd really rather
Stay up later tonight
And paste or paint or colour
Or fly my kite at night
Or …
Rollerskate?
Play hide-and-seek?
Perhaps a pillow fight?

Well, before I go
Just one more thing
My bed is full of bugs
Or maybe we could rock
And have a couple of hugs?

I knew that hugs would work
Now I have to tell you this
I'm really very tired
Here's a good-night kiss.

Football by **George Bainbridge** (UK)

Crowds cheering.
Managers yelling,
Goalkeepers diving,
Nets rustling,
Players kicking,
Bands playing,
Atmosphere building,
Determined team,
Sweaty armpits,
Wingers dribbling,
Strikers heading,
Crowds tensing,
Men betting,
Balls speeding,
Players injured,
Players cursing,
Coaches observing,
Substitutes waiting.

(A winning poem from the Society of Teachers of Speech and Drama poetry writing competition.)

A *Drowning* by Charlotte Trevella

(Age 11 – New Zealand)

The day
   after
a ship's skeleton
  is drifting
  further
     away from land.

Parents
  stand on cliff
  edge
and say:
  'last night's storm.
  Pity.
  some survived though.
  Some.'

At water's
  edge
  children help
  the sea sort
  through
    flotsam and
  wreckage.

Trying on
  waterlogged bonnets
and caps
  until parents shout
'Oi away from
the dead man's
  clothes.'

Dawn light
    brightens,
Tears fall
    like sea water.

Grubs by **Olga Coleman**
(Australian writer now living in New Zealand.)

Grubs! grubs! grubs! grubs!
What a maddening plague we have of grubs!
Our beautiful Poinciana tree
Was ever so lovely – a joy to see!
But to our surprise, in a matter of hours,
They'd gobbled the leaves and even the flowers!

These greedy grubs weren't content with that,
They arched, flipped and wriggled across the mat,
Waved themselves up all the bricks,
So we finally had to get some sticks.
We used our brooms, plus two dustpans,
And filled buckets with water too hot for our hands.

With anger and pleasure we shovelled these grubs,
And rapidly gave them a bath without suds!
They didn't think this a good idea,
So didn't enjoy what we did, I fear.
I've read of battles and many attacks,
But these thousands of grubs can attack down our backs!

This grub has a golden-brown head like a knob,
And he uses it to sway and bob.
If he has any eyes they are so small,
I've looked, but I can't see them at all.
He has two whiskers which move about,
His mouth seems white, but his nose I doubt.

He spits a juice of golden-brown
When I prod and turn him upside down.
His body is colourfully striped
With lines of gold and black and white.
Down both sides there's a dainty design
Of scallops which appear very fine.

His final-rear legs, as he rests on the rail,
Seem a golden-brown horseshoe, and look like a tail.
He has two other sets of legs at the rear,
He grips with these and senses no fear
As he rapidly swings from left to right –
He does many contortions, for he's very bright.

I wonder if you've really looked at a grub?
Or, as you've passed by just given him a stub?
I stared through a magnifier to see
Just how this grub appears to me.
He's beautiful, I must confess –
What a pity he likes to make such a mess!

(This is the Geometric Caterpillar.)

Skin by David Campbell (Australia)

I wonder why
my skin's so thin ...
it has to keep
my insides in!
It also blocks
the nasties out ...
it's something I
can't do without!

It's funny stuff,
it splits and peels,
but if it's cut …
guess what? It heals!
It's one of my
most precious things …
the way it fits,
the way it clings.

A wrinkle here,
a dimple there,
it hugs me tight
just everywhere!
It stays with me
for all I do,
and as I grow
it stretches too!

On leg or arm
or nose or chin
I really love
my skinny skin!

The Bogus-Boo by James Reeves

The Bogus-Boo
Is a creature who
Comes out at night – and why?
He likes the air;
He likes to scare
The nervous passer-by.

Out from the park
At dead of dark
He comes with huffling pad.
If, when alone,
You hear his moan,
'Tis like to drive you mad.

He has two wings,
Pathetic things,
With which he cannot fly.
His tusks look fierce,
Yet could not pierce
The merest butterfly.

He has six ears,
But what he hears
Is very faint and small;
And with the claws
On his eight paws
He cannot scratch at all.

He looks so wise
With his owl-eyes,
His aspect grim and ghoulish;
But truth to tell,
He sees not well
And is distinctly foolish.

This Bogus-Boo,
What can he do
But huffle in the dark?
So don't take fright;
He has no bite
And very little bark.

Santa's Supper in Sunland by **Olga Coleman**

It was Christmas Eve, and the air was so hot
In a land far away where it rains quite a lot.
Santa looked at his watch, and then said with delight,
'I'm early, but thirsty, and crave for a bite.'

He stood on a tropical beach all alone,
The moonbeams shone on a sand-made throne,
And he merrily mused as the glittering waves
Playfully bounced to some nearby caves.

He sat on the grass, 'neath a palm, tall and round,
Then opened some coconuts, there on the ground.
He drank and he drank, and enjoyed every drop,
He tried and he tried, but he just couldn't stop.
By chance, that same day, some campers had sat
On the very same place Santa used as a mat.
A bunch of bananas they'd left in their hurry,
When down came the rain and made them all scurry!

He picked off a few, with a grin of delight,
And had a good feed, as they were quite ripe.
Midnight came all too soon for his rounds to begin,
So he hastily left, feeling full, but not thin.

Whacks and Wickets by **Annette Kosseris** (Australia)

I love sports,
Especially cricket
I'm good at batting
And defending the wicket.

And I can bowl,
And I can catch.
On Saturday
There's a cricket match.

I'll be bowling
And with some luck
I might get someone
Out for a duck!

He'll look surprised
And check his bat,
And the crowd will shout
''Ow zat! ... 'OW ZAT!'

Yeah ...
    I LOVE
        cricket!

The Spider in my Room by **James Tilley**
(A winner from the STSD competition.)

He's gone in a crack.
I don't know when he's coming back
Maybe he's lurking behind my wardrobe
Trying to get out.
But will I shout?
He's maybe under my bed.
Trying to sneak up to my head.
He could be behind my desk,
Having a little rest.
Finally he shouts, 'Yippee I'm out.'

I look at him.
He's very thin.
So I let him out the door!

Hayfever Rap by **Anne Bell** (Australia)

'Ahtishoo!'

Blesshoo –
but I wishoo
would not leave
in pocket or sleeve
the tishoo
that comforts your nose.
When washed with the clothes
it surprisingly grows
into leopard spots
and polka dots
that lovingly cling
to everything
like flakes of falling snow.

I wish it wasn't so.

Assembly by **Anne Bell** (Australia)

Somebody whispered something
and a little titter
skittered and scuttled along the rows
then burrowed under a heap of teachers' frowns.
Nobody spoke.
The hall was huge with silence.
No words fluttered on the empty air,

only dust motes moved
in the curious light
that chinned itself up to the window
and peered through.
Somebody coughed.
Feet shuffled themselves.
The headmaster banged his fist
until the startled lectern jumped with fright.

'You! You down there!
That boy in the green shirt!'
His signpost finger zapped us all,
but nobody moved;
nobody spoke.
Only the titter, feral as anything,
blundered around the room,
seeking escape.

Well, I mean, the school uniform –
it's grey trousers –
and the shirt is green.

Ghost Story by **Bill Scott** (Australia)

There once was a ghost who lived in a tomb
in a place that was murky with horror and gloom,
where gravestones stuck up like a row of bad teeth
concealing the horrors that lay underneath.
As the last stroke of midnight resounded around
the ghost would rise up from his bed underground
and making a noise like a quavering bleat
would leap out of hiding and bite people's feet.

One night Sarah Jenkins was tottering past
who had not washed her feet since the year before last.
The ghost sprang from hiding and with a loud chuckle
sank its ugly green teeth in her left big-toe knuckle.
Sarah, not noticing, wandered away
but the ghost foamed and roared and kept spitting all day.
Even now, around midnight, when white fog lies thick
if you go by that graveyard, just listen a tick
and you'll still hear the sound of the ghost being sick.

The Lion and the Unicorn by **Bill Scott** (Australia)

Once upon a time, a long time ago
lived a unicorn with a spike on his nose.
He had opal eyes and a coat like moonlight,
he could run so fast his shadow couldn't catch him
till he stopped.

He was lovely to look at, but oh! He was nasty!
He'd wait till the others were sleeping soundly,
creep up quietly so they didn't waken
and prod them on the backside with his pointy spike.
'Wow!' they shouted.

Kangaroos leapt and wallabies bellowed.
Wombats dug so he couldn't reach them.
Possums stayed in the tops of gum trees,
snakes and lizards hid among boulders
while the unicorn giggled and sharpened his spike
on sandstone.

One day, Unicorn was running up a mountain.
Under a clump of crimson waratah
he saw a fat, round, furry backside
and heard the sound of somebody snoring
very loudly.

He crept as quiet as a mouse over feathers,
jabbed, then laughed at the yell that followed.
Out of the bushes, faster than a rocket
sprang a huge marsupial lion.
It ate him!

But the lion was not as clever as he thinked –
both him and the unicorn are now extinct.

Super-Spy Dreaming by **Matthew Rodger**
(A winner from the STSD competition.)

I have a dream, perhaps one day
that 'M' would knock to call and say
the world's in peril, we need you fast
a villain's aim – our world to blast
you're the man we need to send
this blackguard's reign – it has to end.
I'd own a Walter PPK
(and keep the neighbour's cat at bay).
Snug and safe, strapped to my chest –
a bulge beneath my PE vest!
An Aston Martin would be mine.
Oh, how my travels would be divine.
Road miles covered in a flash –
(with all the girls I'd be a smash!)

Packed with gadgets, really neat,
(and a quick-release ejector seat).
Flashy clothes – I'd look so cool
designer gear would be the rule.
Dark, slick shades add mystery
disguise, protect, the REAL me!
'Q' would hand me loads of cash,
poison pen – I'd get no trash
I'd need to fly to sunny nations
to find the tyrant's destinations.
Sip Martinis in the heat,
follow clues and act discreet.
What a life I'd lead for sure
what teenager could ask for more?

Mum's voice destroys my reverie,
returns me to reality.
It's time to take a homework break
what drink would I like to partake?
My answer's firm – I hope she heard,
milk 'n' tea ... 'shaken, not stirred.'

Free Rangers by **Max Fatchen** (Australia)

Chooks in the paddock
Chooks ranging free
Boiled eggs for breakfast?
Scrambled for tea?
Chooks in their sandpit
Dust on their breasts
Searching through boxthorns
Looking for nests.

When the sun's shining
In their tin shed
Chooks on their perches
Early to bed.

Noisy chooks cackling
Greet a new day,
Scratching the seedlings
No time to lay.

Chooks busy feeding
Humbly I beg –
Could you just manage
A newly laid egg?

Dorothy Duck by **Colin Thiele**

Just visit our farmyard – and if you're in luck –
Perhaps you may run into Dorothy Duck.
An elegant lady in yellow and white
Whose dress always seems so impeccably right.

She stands by the track in a ladylike pose
And stretches her neck like a rubbery hose,
Then waddles with dignity down to the creek
And floats like a petal, inscrutably meek.

Miss Duck on the water! A picture to hold,
So elegant, upright, sedate and controlled,
Each eye glinting sharply, a bullety bead,
To watch for alarms or a sign of her feed.

But then just as soon as you throw out the wheat,
She comes dashing forwards with splattering feet;
Oh what a mad rush through the mud and the muck –
Disgusting, disgraceful, Miss Dorothy Duck!

For tumbling and stumbling, afraid she'll be late,
Her frantic feet pedalling a furious rate,
With chest to the ground, and tears on her cheek,
She ploughs up the wheat with the scoop of her beak.

A frightful example of how not to feed –
A duck of bad manners and gobble-billed breed –
Still scooping and scraping, a dredge of a duck,
She snoops in the mush and slush of the muck.

But then, having dashed and dithered a treat,
And gobbled each dollop and dirtied her feet,
Devoured demented her desperate feeds ...
She waddles back seeking her pool by the reeds.

And there, I confess, as she preens and careens,
And sails past the sedges and water-weed greens,
I'd give quite a lot, like Tom Sawyer or Huck,
To dabble and dawdle with Dorothy Duck.

A Word of Warning by **Max Fatchen**

Most unkind words can buzz like bees
So do not let them sting me, please.
But kindly words, as you may know
Can fill me with a friendly glow.

The scolding words that come my way
Will make me tend to disobey
While telling me, 'Do that! Do this!'
Such words I much prefer to miss.

No wonder that I turn and flee
When people want a word with me.
I find they're wanting three or four –
Sometimes considerably more.

At any time of night or day
Some people have too much to say.
If words are whizzing in your head
Why not just leave a few unsaid?

School Bus Ballad by **Max Fatchen**

It clattered past the paddocks with petrol-fuming fuss
While cows would gallop, tails aloft,
to race the old school bus.
And down along those country roads it gave a bumpy ride,
A school Mum at the steering wheel and lively kids inside.

It picked up waiting children, their heavy schoolbags slung,
While sheepdogs from verandahs importantly gave tongue.
It backfired like a howitzer and blokes cried,
'Thar' she blows,'
Alarming shearers in the sheds and panicking the crows.

When winter veiled the ranges and the rain beat
like a drum
The old school bus rolled onwards steered by that
dauntless Mum.
It carried on regardless of heat and dust and mud,
It once outraced a bushfire and struggled through a flood.

The old bus swerved and rattled and took some
careful turning,
Depositing its precious load at local seats of learning,
The sums, the reading and the rest,
how pupils' knowledge soared
And when the day was over, they clambered back aboard.

This transport now long obsolete has met its rusty fate
but there's a local legend for those that stay out late,
That, from a nearby wrecking yard a ghostly bus will glide
A school Mum at the steering wheel and lively kids inside.

The Calf by **Thomas Hardy** (UK)

You may have seen, in road or street,
At times, when passing by,
A creature with bewildered bleat
Behind a milcher's tail, whose feet
Went pit-pat. That was I.

Whether we are of Devon kind,
Shorthorns or Herefords,
We are in general of one mind
That in the human race we find
Our masters and our lords.

When grown-up (if they let me live)
And in a dairy-home,
I may less wonder and misgive
Than now, and get contemplative,
And never wish to roam.

And in some fair stream, taking sips,
May stand through summer noons,
With water dribbling from my lips
And rising halfway to my hips,
And babbling pleasant tunes.

To a Cow by **M. James** (UK)

They took your calf away last night,
So that is why you moo
And all the beasts in sympathy
Mourn from the field with you!

Commiseration flows from me
It flows from every part
As lying still I hear that low
From out your bovine heart.

Maternal anguish racks your frame
And yet you cannot weep,
Just bellow sadly to the stars –
But please, I want some sleep.

At Day-Close in November by **Thomas Hardy**

The ten hours' light is abating,
And a late bird wings across,
Where the pines, like waltzers waiting,
Give their black heads a toss.

Beech leaves, that yellow the noon-time,
Float past like specks in the eye;
I set every tree in my June time,
And now they obscure the sky.

And the children who ramble through here
Conceive that there never has been
A time when no tall trees grew here,
That none will in time be seen.

Three Songs from Shakespeare's *The Tempest*:

1) Come unto these yellow sands,
   And then take hands.
   Curtsied when you have and kissed,
   The wild waves whist,
   Foot it featly here and there
   And sweet sprites bear
   The burden. Hark, hark!

   Hark, hark! I hear
   The strain of strutting Chanticleer
   cry –
   cock-a-diddle-dow!

2. Full fathom five thy father lies;
   Of his bones are coral made;
   Those are pearls that were his eyes;
   Nothing of him that doth fade
   But doth suffer a sea-change
   Into something rich and strange.
   Sea-nymphs hourly ring his knell.
   Hark now I hear them.
   Ding – dong bell.

3. Where the bee sucks, there suck I;
   In a cowslip's bell I lie;
   There I couch when owls do cry;
   On the bat's back I do fly
   After summer merrily.
   Merrily, merrily, shall I live now,
   Under the blossom that hangs on the bough.

To a Butterfly by William Wordsworth

I've watch'd you now a full half-hour,
Self-poised upon that yellow flower:
And, little Butterfly! indeed
I know not if you sleep or feed.
How motionless! – not frozen seas
More motionless! – and then
What joy awaits you, when the breeze
Hath found you out among the trees,
And calls you forth again!

This plot of orchard-ground is ours;
My trees they are, my Sister's flowers,
Here rest your wings when they are weary;
Here lodge as in a sanctuary!
Come often to us, fear no wrong;
Sit near us on the bough!
We'll talk of sunshine and of song,
And summer days, when we were young;
Sweet childish days, that were as long
As twenty days are now.

There's a Toad in the Road at Piccadilly by **John Whitworth**

There's a toad in the Road at Piccadilly
Eros is cross and looking silly.
O toad romantic
Corybantic
Flaunting in the neon glow
Jaunting on jurassic toe.

Toad florescent
Erubescent
Ululating by the gutter
Coruscating through the clutter.

Dancing toad
Entrancing toad
Crooning a reptilian sonnet
In your tam o'shanter bonnet.

Toad poetic
Toad balletic
Skimming through department stores
With a rose between your jaws,
Twinkling down the lighted street,
Toad your eyes are sad and sweet,
Toad my life is incomplete.

I, incessantly lamenting,
Watch your disappearing feet,
Weeping at this strange absenting.

Toad your heart is made of granite,
Your disdain is unrelenting,
Softly to a fading planet,
I alone intone an ode.
There's a toad in the road at Piccadilly
Eros is cross and looking silly.

THE INTERMEDIATE COLLECTION

The material in this section is substantial enough to allow students to explore the writers' ideas and intentions and to bring their own interpretation in performance. Themes, characters, situations and moods will all be found in pieces of greater complexity and demand, yet, the emphasis remains securely on the ability to relate a personal or universal story. The selection covers a wide range of styles and use of language and, when selecting pieces for performance, it should be possible to respond to the quality of the material and demonstrate a developing number of performance skills.

Candidates for grades 4–5 examinations will find it helpful to engage with much of the poetry, drama and prose in this section. It is drawn from some of the earliest written sources of world literature as well as from important contemporary authors. Much of the material reflects recent rediscovery of universal themes enshrined in stories and legends from diverse cultures, but there is also a substantial body of work that investigates and reflects upon the small details of modern living. Once again, there is an opportunity to use the following pieces in a variety of ways: they are, in no sense, 'set pieces', but are to be used as a resource for students who are progressively mastering the arts of performance and who are seeking stimulating texts.

Intermediate Drama:

The drama pieces in this section are from a very wide range of cultures and many of them are dramatisations of ancient stories. Some of the material is suitable for use in acting, performance arts or speech and drama, where either individual or group performance is required. You should feel free to adapt the texts to your own needs.

The Mahabharata is the longest poem ever written. It is about fifteen times as long as the Bible and was written in Sanskrit, one of the languages of ancient India, more than two thousand years ago. In recent years, Jean-Claude Carrière has made a translation that formed the basis of a stage production by the remarkable director, Peter Brook. Here is an extract from the opening moments:

Extract from *Mahabharata*

A BOY of about twelve enters. He goes towards a little pool. Then a MAN appears. He is thin, wearing a muddy loincloth, his feet bare and dirty. He sits thoughtfully on the ground and, noticing the BOY, he signals him to come closer. The BOY approaches, slightly fearful. The MAN asks him:

VYASA Do you know how to write?

BOY No, why?   [*The MAN is silent for a moment before saying:*

VYASA I've composed a great poem. I've composed it all, but nothing is written. I need someone to write down what I know.

BOY What's your name?

VYASA Vyasa.

BOY What's your poem about?

VYASA It's about you.

BOY Me?

VYASA Yes, it's the story of your race, how your ancestors were born, how they grew up, how a vast war arose. It's the poetical history of mankind. If you listen carefully, at the end you'll be someone else. For it's a pure as glass, yet nothing is omitted. It washes away faults, it sharpens the brain and it gives long life.

> [*Suddenly, the BOY points, indicating a strange form approaching in the distance*

BOY Who's that?

> [*It is someone with an elephant's head and a man's body, who comes strutting towards them. He has writing materials in his hand. VYASA greets him warmly*

52

VYASA Ganesha! Welcome.

BOY You're Ganesha?

GANESHA Rumour has it that you're looking for a scribe for the Poetical History of Mankind. I'm at your service.

BOY You're really Ganesha?

GANESHA In person.

BOY Why do you have an elephant's head?

GANESHA Don't you know?

BOY No.

GANESHA If I've got to tell my story too, we'll never finish.

BOY Please.

GANESHA Right. I am the son of Parvati, the wife of Shiva.

BOY The wife of the great god, Shiva?

GANESHA Himself. But Shiva's not my father. My mother did it alone.

BOY How did she manage?

GANESHA It's not easy. To cut a long story short, when I arrived in this world, I was already a fine, sturdy boy, just about your age. One day, my mother told me to guard the door of the house. She wanted to take a bath. 'Let no one in,' she said. An instant later, Shiva was standing in front of me, wanting to come into the house, his house. I blocked the way. Shiva did not know me – I'd only just been born – so he said, 'Out of my way! It's an order. This is my house.' I answered, 'My mother told me to let no one in, so I'm letting no one in.' Shiva was furious. He called up his most ferocious cohorts. He commanded them to flush me out, but I sent them flying. My force was superhuman. I blazed, I glittered, I exploded – horde after horde of demons withdrew in shame, for I was defending my mother. Shiva had only one way left: cunning. He slipped behind me and suddenly he chopped off my head. My mother's anger had no limits. She threatened to destroy all the powers of heaven and smash the sky into tiny splinters. Shiva, to calm her down, ordered a head to be put on me as quickly as possible, the head of the first creature to come by. It was an elephant. So there we are. I'm Ganesha, the bringer of peace. [*He positions himself with great care and says to* VYASA] I'm ready. You can begin. But I warn you: my hand can't stop once I start to write. You must dictate without a single pause.

VYASA   And you, before putting anything down, you must understand the sense of what I say.

GANESHA   Count on me. [*A silence falls and lasts a few moments*] We're expecting someone?

VYASA   No.

GANESHA   So ...?

VYASA   There's something secret about a beginning. I don't know how to start.

GANESHA   May I offer a suggestion?

VYASA   You're most welcome to.

GANESHA   As you claim to be the author of the poem, how about beginning with yourself?

Marouf the Cobbler is another ancient story, this time drawn from Middle-Eastern culture. It was originally passed down by oral tradition, but first became known in English through a translation known as *Thousand And One Nights*, by Sir Richard Burton. The stage version included here was made by the Caravan of Dreams Theatre, an international actors' ensemble founded in San Francisco.

Extract from *Marouf the Cobbler*

In this next scene, DUNYA, MAROUF very young wife, tries to elicit the truth from her husband:

SCENE 17

DUNYA   O my beloved,
    O coolth of my eyes, O fruit of my vitals,
    Allah never desolate me with your loss,
    Nor time sunder us two, you and me.
    Indeed, the love of you has homed in my heart,
    The fire of passion has consumed my liver,

Nor will I ever forsake you,
Or go against you.
But I would have you tell me the truth,
For the shifts of falsehood do not profit,
Nor do they gain credit for all seasons.
How long will you impose on my father and lie to him?
I fear that your affair he discovered to him,
Before we can devise some device,
And he will lay violent hands upon you.
So acquaint me with the facts of the case,
Nothing shall happen to you except to gladden you.
When you have spoken truly,
Don't fear that harm will befall you.
How often will you declare you are a merchant, rich,
And have a caravan?
For a long time now you say my caravan, my caravan!
But no sign appears of your goods,
Your face shows your anxiety.
Now if there is no value in your words,
Tell me, and I will contrive you a contrivance
So that you come off safe, *inshallah*!

MAROUF I will tell you the truth,
    Then do what you will.

DUNYA Speak, and look you speak truly,
    For truth is the ark of safety,
    And beware of lying,
    It dishonours the liar.

MAROUF Know then, my lady,
    That I am no merchant and have no caravan;
    No, I was but a shoemaker in my own country,
    And had a wife called Fatimah the Dung
    Who drove me out of the City into the desert,
    A Changed One, took me to the top of yonder mountain,
    Ali I found here, he told me to say I had plenty
    Of whatever anyone asked me about, and so –

DUNYA Truly you are clever
In the practice of lying and imposture!
MAROUF O my lady, may Allah the Mighty preserve you
To veil sins and countervail chagrins!
DUNYA Look, you imposed upon my father,
And deceived him by your deluding boasts,
So that out of greed for gain
He married me to you.
Then you squandered his wealth,
And the Vizir bears you a grudge for this.
Many times he spoke against you,
Calling you a liar and imposter.
But my father would not listen to him,
Because the Vizir had tried to wed me
But I would not consent to it.
However, time has stretched out, my father doubted,
And he told me, make him confess.
So I have made you to confess
And what was covered is discovered.
Now my father proposes mischief for you because of this,
But you have become my man,
And I will not go against you.
If I told my father what I've learned from you,
That you impose on Kings' daughters and squander wealth,
He would slay you without a doubt.
Then it would be noised among the people
That I had married such a man, and my honor be smirched.
Furthermore, if he kill you,
Probably he would require me to marry that other,
And I will never consent to such a thing,
No, not though I die!
So rise, dress in a Mameluke's dress,
Take these fifty thousand dinars of my money,
Mount a swift steed,
And get you to land beyond the boundaries

Of my Father's rule.
Then make yourself a merchant,
Send me a letter by private courier,
That I may know where you live,
So that I can send you all my hand can garner.
Thus your wealth shall wax great,
And if my father die, I'll send for you,
You can return with respect and honor,
And if we die, you or I,
And go to the mercy of Allah the Most Great,
Resurrection will unite us.
This, then, is the right way:
And while we both live and are well
I will not cease to send you letters and monies.
Arise before dawn and vengeance light upon your head!

David Campton, who died very recently, was one of Britain's most remarkable playwrights. Much of his early success was achieved with plays designed to be performed 'In-The-Round' and he went on to write a large number of plays for all-female casts or for casts in which the characters could be of either sex. In the following extract from the opening of his *Life and Death of Almost Everybody*, he explores some of the ideas of creation surrounding the stage itself and its relation to life:

Extract from *The Life and Death of Almost Everybody*

An empty stage. House lights on in the auditorium. Working light on over the stage. A MAN with a brush appears and starts to sweep the stage. After a while, he pauses.

SWEEPER Dust. Dust. Every particle guaranteed to last. If the world went bang, and blew us all across the universe, there'd still be dust – drifting across the light years to settle on some other planet: piling up in corners, waiting for a brush. Listen to it.

Just listen. Patter-patter. Where I've just cleaned. Turn your back, and it's landed again. Leave it a year, and it's piled up an inch thick. Come again in a thousand years and you'll find it knee-deep. You don't believe me? Come back in a thousand years and check. What's that? In a thousand years we'll all be dust? Let's have a grand reunion then. Let's have fun with some other poor twit. Patter-patter. Where he's just been with his brush. 'Don't worry, chum,' we'll tell him. 'Join the party.' ... Mind you, I'm not claiming that's an original thought. I never have original thoughts now. A long time ago I thought that I might: then I discovered they'd all been thought before. They seem to float in the air. Like dust. [*Sweeps in silence for a few strokes.*] I'm paid for this. My duties were carefully detailed when I was taken on. All the musts and must nots. Keep the stage clean, I was told. Actors have to fall down on that stage. They roll round when they fight, die, make love ... Sometimes even in the plays. A dirty floor distresses the wardrobe mistress ... Well, if you've nothing better to do, you can watch me. See? That's how it's done. Nice, easy movements. Professional. If you want to learn how to use a brush, I know my job backwards. [*Sweeps.*] This is the way I like a stage. Bare. Anything can happen on a bare stage. Whenever I see a bare stage I get an itch. I want to ... Beg pardon. I was somewhat transported. Besides, the Manager said I mustn't. [*Sweeps.*] You leave the stage alone, the Manager warned me. Clean it, yes. Leave it as spotless as a guardsman's badge; but that's the limit of your involvement. You regard the stage as sacred, he instructed me. With an empty stage you can be tempted to play God, and that's a high-voltage game. He dissuaded me. A stage can be a source of danger. Sweep it, yes. Scrub it, yes. Dust out the corners if the mood moves you. But, for pity's sake, don't go tampering with it. It's a keyhole for peering into the unknown. But don't you go opening any doors, he cautioned me. You might let something out you can't push back. You're a good man with a brush, he flattered me. You stick to your brush. A brush is safe.

Not like a stage. You leave that stage alone, or else, he threatened me. Don't you go playing God, he shouted at me. [*Sweeps.*] So I didn't ... When you start to create something, it's the audience that won't let you drop it. Nobody told me that: I worked it out for myself. I can watch, can't I? I can see what goes on. It's the audience. I never had an audience before. I never ... But the Manager said I mustn't. [*Sweeps.*] But a tiny idea couldn't matter so much. Not as long as I made it quite clear who's in control.

So try to imagine it's darker there, and lighter here. Imagine. Please. Imagine. [*The lights over the audience dim out. A pool of light over the SWEEPER in the centre of the stage comes up. The working light goes out.*] That's better. That's what imagination can do for you. Now something really big. A man and a woman. I never tried with a man and a woman before. That's really taking a chance. Men and women have minds of their own. The Manager told me so. That's what makes them different. That's what makes them dangerous. Well, I shan't give them minds, so there's nothing to be afraid of. They'll just do as they're told. And if they don't do as they're told, I can always unthink them – now. This is the most fantastic trick I ever pulled. You don't believe I can do it, do you? Well, don't think about me. Think about them. A Man and a Woman. [*A YOUNG MAN and YOUNG WOMAN emerge from the shadows at the back of the stage. They are dressed in a neutral costume. Their faces are expressionless. Their bodies are quite relaxed, but equally expressionless. They walk into the light, and stand waiting – two mindless bodies.*] That's some creation, that is.

One of the oldest types of drama in English is found in the 'cycles' of plays telling stories from the Bible and were performed in medieval Europe. The following short play comes from the cycle presented in the English city of York and this slightly modernised version was part of a revival of these plays in the twentieth century.

Some of the language may seem very archaic, but you will find it very accessible in performance:

The Nativity

The Characters:

MARY

JOSEPH

The Tile Thatchers' Play

[JOSEPH and MARY walk together

JOSEPH All mighty God in Trinity,
  I pray thee, Lord, for thy great might,
  Unto thy simple servants see,
  Here is this place where we are pight
  In lonely case.
  Lord, grant us good harbour this night
  Within this place.
  For in great need now are we stead.
  As thou thyself in sooth may see;
  For here is neither clothes nor bed,
  And we are weak and all-weary,
  And fain would rest.
  Most gracious Lord, for thy mercy
  Guide us the best.
MARY God will us guide, full well wit ye;
  Therefore, Joseph, be of good cheer.
  For in this place born will he be
  That shall save us from sorrows here
  Both even and morn.
  Sir, wit ye well the time is near
  He shall be born.
JOSEPH Then had we better bide here still,
  Here in this same place all this night.
MARY Yes, sir; forsooth, it is God's will.

60

JOSEPH Then would I fain we had some light,
  Whate'er befall
  It waxes right dark to my sight,
  And cold withal.
  I will go get us light this tide,
  And fuel find with me to bring.   *[JOSEPH goes*

MARY Almighty God you rule and guide;
  Now in my soul great joy have I,
  I am all clad in comfort clear;
  Now will be born of my body
  Both God and man together here –
  Blest might he be!   *[The CHILD is born*
  Jesu! My son that is so dear –
  Now born is he.
  Hail, my Lord God! Hail, Prince of Peace!
  Hail, my Father and Hail, my son!
  Hail, sovereign strong all sins to cease!
  Hail, God and man on earth in one!
  Hail, through whose might
  All this world once was first begun.
  Darkness and light.
  Son, as I am simple subject to thine,
  Vouchsafe, Sweet Son, I pray to thee,
  I may take thee in these arms of mine,
  And in this poor weed array thee.
  Grant me thy bliss,
  As I am thy Mother chosen to be
  In truthfulness.

JOSEPH enters from another place

JOSEPH Ah Lord, what! The weather is cold,
  The fellest freeze that e'er did I feel.
  I pray God help them that is old
  Or weak or infirm any deal,

So may I say.
Now good God be thou my shield,
As thou best may.
Ah Lord God! What light is this.
That comes shining thus suddenly?
I cannot say, as I have bliss.
When I come home unto Mary,
I will ask her.
Ah! here be food, for now come I.

MARY Ye are welcome, sir.

JOSEPH Say, Mary, daughter, what cheer with thee?

MARY Right good, Joseph, as hath been aye.

JOSEPH O Mary, what sweet thing's that on thy knee?

MARY It is my son, the sooth to say,
So good and mild.

[JOSEPH takes the CHILD

Well is me that I bide this day.
To see this child.
Now welcome, flower fairest of hue,
I'll worship thee with main and might.
Hail, my Maker! Hail, Christ Jesu!
Hail, royal King, Root of all right!
Hail, Saviour!
Hail, my Lord, lender of light!
Hail, blessed flower!
Now, Lord, that all the world shall win,
To thee my son it is I say.
Here is no bed to lay thee in;
Therefore, my dear son, I thee pray
Since it is so
Here in this crib I might thee lay,
Humble and low.

[Lays CHILD in the manger

The myths of the Native Americans are a rich source of poetic explanations for the mystery of creation. In this extract from a stage version of some of these stories, we learn how the world came to be known as 'Turtle Island':

Extract from *Turtle Island*

(A play by Ken Pickering)

WISE WOMAN Listen all of you to what I have to say.

[From this point the story is acted out as it is told

In the beginning there was nothing. Maheo, the Great Spirit, lived in a void.

MAHEO [*appearing above*] I look around but there is nothing to see. I listen. There is nothing to hear. I am alone in nothingness. I am not lonely, for I am a Universe in myself; but I feel that my power must serve some purpose. What use is power if it is not employed to make a world and people to live in it?

WISE WOMAN With his power, Maheo created a great water, like a lake, but salty.

MAHEO Out of this lake I can bring all life. It is cool and tangy in the darkness of nothingness. There must be water beings: fish swimming in the deep water. And I will make mud and sand so that my lake has a bottom: mussels, snails and crawfish shall live there. Let us also create something that lives on the surface of the water. I should like to see the things that have been created.

WISE WOMAN And so it was. Light began to glow and spread. First bleached in the East, then golden and strong in the middle of the sky ... until it extended all round the horizon.

MAHEO How very beautiful it all is!

SNOWGOOSE [*looking to where she thinks MAHEO is*] I do not see you, Maheo, but I know that you exist. I don't know where you are ... but I think you must be somewhere, or perhaps everywhere. Listen, Maheo, this is good water that you have made and we enjoy living on it, but birds are not like fish. We sometimes get tired of swimming – sometimes we would like to get out of the water.

MAHEO I hear you, Snowgoose. Very well then, fly! How beautiful their
wings are in the light.

LOON Maheo! You have made the light and the broad sky for us to fly
in. You have made the cool water for us to swim in. I know it
sounds ungrateful to want something else – but when we are
tired of swimming and tired of flying, we should like a dry, solid
place where we could walk and rest. Please give us a place to
build our nests, Maheo.

MAHEO Well, so be it. But to make such a place I shall need your help.
I have already made the water, the light, the sky-air and the water
creatures. My powers will only allow me to make four things by
myself ...

BIRDS Tell us how we can help you. We are ready to do what you say.

MAHEO Let the biggest and swiftest try to find land first!

SNOWGOOSE I am ready to fly and to try.

MAHEO Well, what have you brought us?

SNOWGOOSE [*sadly*] Nothing, nothing, I brought nothing back.

LOON I will try.

MALLARD I can move swiftly across the surface of water. I will try.

MAHEO I am very much afraid you have failed, Mallard!

COOT Listen, Maheo, listen, everybody. I know I am very small, but as all
these swift birds have failed, may I try?

MAHEO Certainly, Sister Coot.

COOT Maheo, when I put my head beneath the water it seems to me
that I can see something there, far below. Perhaps I can swim
down to it. I know I cannot fly or drive like my sisters and
brothers, all I can do is swim. But I will swim down as best I can
and go as deep as possible. May I try, please, Maheo?

MAHEO Little Sister, no one can do more than her best and I have asked
help of all the water peoples. Certainly you shall try. Swimming may
be better than diving after all. Try and see what you can do.

COOT Thank you, Maheo!

WISE WOMAN The Coot was gone a long, long, long, time.

BIRD ONE [*looking down into the water*] I can see a tiny dark spot. I think
it is rising.

BIRD TWO It's still rising.

BIRD THREE It is the Coot.

BIRD FOUR Sister Coot is swimming up from the bottom of the lake!

MAHEO So. I shall become visible. Give me what you have brought. Now place it in my hand. Go, little Sister, thank you. You have brought me a small ball of mud. May it protect you always!

WISE WOMAN And so it was, and is: for the Coot's flesh still tastes of mud and neither man nor woman will eat it.

MAHEO [*rolling the ball of mud in his hands*] Come and help me again, water peoples. I must put this somewhere. One of you must let me place it on your back.

FIRST VOICE I'm too small.

SECOND VOICE We fish are too narrow and our fins will cut the mud to pieces.

THIRD VOICE We've got solid backs, but we live at the bottom of the lake. Turtle, do you think you could carry the weight on your back?

MAHEO This is very worrying: there is only one water creature left. Grandmother, you can help me?

TURTLE I am very old and slow, but I will try.

MAHEO I will pile this mud on your back until I have made a hill.

[*Does so*

WISE WOMAN And the hill grew and spread until Grandmother Turtle was hidden from sight.

MAHEO So be it. Let the earth be known as our Mother and let the Grandmother who carries the earth be the only creature who is at home beneath the water and above the ground, for she shall carry the weight of the whole world and its peoples on her back.

A VOICE All her descendents will have to walk very slowly!

TURTLE We cannot all be fleet of foot. Nor do we wish to be!

ANOTHER VOICE But, Maheo; there may be earth now as well as water; but this earth is barren.

MAHEO You are right: the earth should be fruitful. Help me my power, let her begin to bear life.

WISE WOMAN And so it was that the plants and fruits and flowers were
the gifts that the earth offered back to the Great Spirit, Maheo.
CHIEF TWO And all these things are our brothers and sisters. You have
told your story well, Wise Woman!

[*Song:*] *The Perfumed Flowers are our Sisters*

The perfumed flowers are our sisters,
The deer, the horse, the great eagle,
These, these are our brothers.
We are part of the earth,
And the earth is part of us,
For the earth is our mother.
The rocky crests and the meadows,
The body heat of the pony,
These are part of one family.
We are sustained by the earth,
The earth looks for our love,
For the earth is our mother.

Gulliver's Travels, written in the very early years of the eighteenth
century by Jonathan Swift, have been a constant source of fascination
to readers of all ages. The book has been made into several films,
plays and musicals, but its biting, political satire is often overlooked.
In the country of Lilliput, inhabited by tiny people less than
six-inches high, there is a fierce political debate over which end of a
boiled egg one should open first, and this leads to religious hatred
and war.

In this extract from a version made for the German Theatre Company,
Westfälisches Landestheater, Gulliver has just been shipwrecked. You
may like to know that, in the original production, the role of Gulliver
was played by a young woman.

Extract from *Gulliver in Lilliput*

(by Ken Pickering)

A bare stage. Towards the centre there is a raised area.

Enter GULLIVER staggering with exhaustion

GULLIVER [*breathing heavily*] Oh ... oh ... I'm so ... tired ... so exhausted ... all that swimming ... and the ship wrecked ... totally wrecked. [*Sinks down to the ground*] I think all my friends must have been drowned ... swept away. There's only me alive now ... just me, Gulliver. [*Looking around*] What is this place? Where am I? I'm just too tired to explore. I must sleep ... must sleep ... sleep

> [*Gradually sleeps and sinks into deep snoring. PAUSE. GULLIVER snores even louder and then begins to awake*]

Ah, what a sleep ... I was dreaming [*tries to sit up*]. Ow! OW! ... What's this, I can't move my head ... it's stuck ... my hair is stuck to the ground ... and my hands and arms ... what's happening? I can't move ANYTHING. OUCH! Something's pulling my hair. [*Very slowly*] If I could just turn my head perhaps ... OW ... no, I'd better lie completely still on my back. The trouble is ... I can only look up and the sun's in my eyes. Now what am I supposed to do? Just lie still, Gulliver and THINK. How did this happen? Am I stuck with glue ... or ... no ... I can see now ... if I just look down ... I can see them all over my body ... hundreds of tiny ropes fastening me to the ground ... and my hair ... there are pegs holding my hair down.

Wait a minute ... can I feel something moving ... yes, it's coming up my left leg ... I hope it's not a rat! It's coming close to my chest! [*Exclaiming loudly*] WHAT ... I don't believe this! It was a tiny man ... only about six-inches high. I think I saw several of them and they all ran away. I know ... must speak more quietly ... all those little people falling off me: it must be like falling down a mountain. All right ... I didn't mean to frighten you ... you can come back. Good heavens ... there's about forty of them ... I've never seen anything like it ... I can feel them coming back ... climbing up ... they're so small ... and they've got bows and arrows ready to shoot at me ... I must be careful of my eyes. There's one right up near my face ... he's lifting his hand as if to say 'hello'. No, don't do that ... it tickles ... It will make me blink or sneeze!

[*Struggling to free left arm*] If I could just ... get ... my arm free ... [*pulls*]. Done it! That's better [*feeling hair*], now I can feel how they have fixed my hair ... perhaps I could ... OW ... I can move my head [*looking towards audience*]. Look at you all ... hundreds of you looking at me! I'll catch one of you ... agh ... missed ... he just wriggled through my fingers ... it's OK ... I'm not going to hurt you. [*Suddenly shielding head with hands*] OW ... OW ... OW ... OW ... that hurts! OW ... arrows ... sticking in my hands, like needles ... and my face. STOP IT!! I can see what some of them are trying to do ... stick spears into me ... thank goodness I'm wearing this thick jerkin. They can't pierce that.

I'd better stop struggling and be friendly. I'll lie absolutely still. [*To AUDIENCE*] Will you all please tell me when the little people are coming back?

Here is another moment of drama that begins with a shipwreck. In Shakespeare's *The Tempest*, the King and all his court are shipwrecked and scattered around an island. Trinculo, the jester, comes across Caliban, one of the island's few original inhabitants, trying to hide under his 'gaberdine' or heavy cloak.

Extract from: *The Tempest*

Enter CALIBAN carrying a burden of wood

CALIBAN All the infections that the sun sucks up
    From bogs, fen, flats, on Prosper fall, and make him
    By inch-meal a disease. His spirits hear me,
    And yet I needs must curse. But they'll not pinch,

Fright me with urchin-shows, pitch me i' the mire,
Nor lead me like a firebrand in the dark
Out of my way, unless he bid 'em; but
For every trifle are they set upon me;
Sometimes like apes, that mow and chatter at me,
And after bite me; then like hedgehogs, which
Lie tumbling in my barefoot way, and mount
Their pricks at my footfall; sometimes am I
All wound with adders, who with their cloven tongues
Do hiss me to madness.

Enter TRINCULO

Lo, now, lo!
Here comes another spirit of his, and to torment me
For bringing wood in slowly. I'll fall flat;
Perchance he will not mind me.

TRINCULO Here's neither bush nor shrub to bear off any weather at all. And another storm brewing; I hear it sing i' the wind. Yond same black cloud, yond huge one, looks like a foul bombard that would shed his liquor. If it should thunder as it did before, I know not where to hide my head: yond same cloud cannot choose but fall by pailfuls. [*Notices CALIBAN*] What have we here, a man or a fish? Dead or alive? A fish, he smells like a fish; a very ancient and fish-like smell; a kind of ... not of the newest poor-John; a strange fish. Were I in England now, as once I was, and had but this fish painted, not a holiday fool there but would give a piece of silver. There would this monster make a man; any strange beast there makes a man; when they will not give a doit to relieve a lame beggar, they will lay out ten to see a dead Indian. Legged like a man, and his fins like arms; [*Feels CALIBAN*] warm o' my troth! I do now let loose my opinion, hold it no longer: this is no fish, but an islander that hath lately suffered by a thunderbolt. [*More thunder*] Alas, the storm is come again. My best way is to creep under his gaberdine; there is no other

shelter hereabout. Misery acquaints a man with strange
bedfellows; I will here shroud till the dregs of the storm be past.

[*He hides under* CALIBAN'*s cloak*

The writing of very short plays or monologues has become an
important art form in itself and collections of such pieces are often
excellent sources for use in auditions and exams. Here is an extract
from the short play *Return to Sender*, by the American playwright Joseph
McNair Stover, taken from a collection of his plays entitled *Hard Boiled
and other Brief Encounters*:

Extract from *Return to Sender*

RALPH, *a* MAIL CARRIER *(or Postman) has just arrived at a house to deliver
some mail but finds its occupant up a ladder. We can only hear the occupant's
voice, but when the telephone rings in his house he asks* RALPH *to answer it.*

CARRIER [*into phone*] Yes, he is. Up on a ladder, so he can't come in
right now. Hmm? Ralph. No, I'm sure you don't know me. The
mail carrier. To answer the phone. No, it's not something I
usually do. What? I am not a burglar! Look, he asked me to
come in and ... What? Yes, I'm sure he can't come to the phone
right now. Well ... Perhaps. [*Listens. Looks around as though
obeying instructions.*] Yes, I'm standing right in front of it.
[*Hesitates*] I can't do that. But what would it look like if he came
in? [*Peers out of doorway*] Oh, all right.

[MAIL CARRIER *goes through desk's
principal drawer. Sets items he finds on
desktop*

No, I've found a chequebook, a photograph, a ring box, a card
and a box of chocolates, but no slip of paper with an address on
it. [*Looks at photograph*] I must say, if this photograph is of you,
he's a lucky man. Why would I lie? No, not too fat. No, of course
not. Yes, diets are hard to keep. No, I wouldn't blame you a bit.
Not at all. Yes, a good slice of cheesecake is very hard to resist.

Oh! ... The whole cake. Well, judging by this photo you can afford to splurge once in a while. No, I'm just being honest. No, I'm not. No, I'm not. No, I'm not. Honestly. Yes. Very sincere. Why would I? I don't even know you. There'd be no reason to flatter you. You're welcome. Well, thank you. You have a nice voice, too. Yes, I am. Yes, I am. Yes, I am. What? The ring box? [*Picks up ring box and examines it*] Oh, I don't know, just an ordinary ring box. I don't know if I should. How do you know he wouldn't mind? No, I don't know how he is, that's just the point. Really? [*Peers through the doorway*] Doesn't seem the type. [*Abruptly*] No, of course not. No, I would never question anybody's taste in men. Yes. Okay, well, I apologize. Thank you. Yes, thank you very much. No, I don't believe you're high strung. He does? Why? [Puzzled] What? Where? Uh-huh. Mmm. No, absolutely not. No, antlers definitely should not be left in a place like that. Well, yes. Yes, I can imagine your surprise ... especially that late at night. No, I don't blame you one bit. No, screaming would be a very normal reaction. You're welcome. Yes, you're quite welcome. Oh, yes, the ring box. Well, if you're sure about this? [*Opens box*] Wow! [*Responds to phone*]. No, I did not injure myself. No, no. There's not an antler in sight. I said, 'Wow'. Yes. Well, because it's impressive; quite a diamond. Yes, a large diamond; quite a ring. Yes, definitely an engagement ring. [*Holds phone away from ear as though in pain. Speaks into mouthpiece*] I'm very glad you're so excited. Congratulations.

Isadora Duncan was one of the pioneers of modern dance. She was greatly inspired by a sense of liberty and freedom and by the events of the Russian Revolution that she witnessed at first hand. This scene comes from a modern 'cycle' of plays written for the Quaker Youth Theatre by a team of playwrights celebrating the end of the twentieth century and tracing some of the events which would have affected a child born in 1900. This section from *The House of Parables* was written by Ken Pickering:

Extract from *The House of Parables*

ISADORA enters and slowly stretching she begins to dance

[*CHORUS*] Dance, Isadora, dance to freedom,
Flowing free to a promised land;
Limbs and spirit shun restriction,
Tired modes and rules are banned.
Come up to the mountain top:
All the plains of imagination,
The search for forms of expression,
Milk and honey of new hope.
Stretch out ... to the horizon:
Let my people go!
Plagues of oppression,
Plagues of repression,
The fire in the burning bush.
Is the fire of the new spirit:
Let the people go!

[*As ISADORA pauses in her dance there is the sound of the singing of the*
Internationale *and a great procession of banner-bearing people enters*]

ISADORA [*watching*] The first of May in Moscow was a wonderful sight.
The streets were like crimson roses. Thousands of men, women
and children, with red handkerchiefs about their heads and red
flags in their hands, swept by singing the *Internationale.* All these
people had lived for four years on black bread and grey rice, but
I fancy that the first of May meant more joy to them than every
year of good feeling under the Czar ...
[*They all sing and she dances to the singing*
ALL   The Earth shall rise on new foundations,
We have been naught, we shall be all.
ISADORA [*pausing in her dance as the procession moves away*] ... I wished with

all my heart that this song would be radioed around the whole Earth ... [*the music builds to a great climax ... she continues dancing and calling out in ecstacy*] I salute the birth of the future community of International Love ... for the first time in my life I feel I can stretch out my arms and breathe ... I have danced the Revolution!

> [*She continues to dance ... after a while there is another pause. She rests and sits or stands very naturally with her loose clothes casually draped on her body*]

If my art is symbolic of one thing, it is symbolic of the freedom of woman and her emancipation from the hidebound conventions that are the warp and woof of (New England) Puritanism ... [*lying down almost languidly*] ... to expose one's body is art: concealment is vulgar. [*Standing and addressing the* AUDIENCE *directly*] I want to free the audience from the chains that bind them ... I see before me shackled ... chained by Puritanism, enslaved and hidebound in mind and body ... they want to be free ... they cry out for someone to loose their chains ... [*she dances on*]. Yes, I am a revolutionist ... all true artists are revolutionists. [*She dances on and as she does, she is joined by other* DANCERS. *Finally, she gathers them around her and she speaks to them.*] There are many who think that life is a series of extremely boring habits which they call virtues. I do not believe in putting chains and padlocks on life. Life is an experience, an adventure, it is an expression. Most Americans are hypnotised by the wrong idea of life, brought to this country by the Puritans ... [*as she is about to dance again*] ... and I hate charity! Rich men work women blind in sweatshops and then endow eye hospitals!

> [*She runs off and the dancers follow*

As we have seen, the short monologue for the stage has become an art form in itself. It is really a complete play in miniature. The next example is by the young Irish playwright Sharon McCoy, from her collection *Feminine Zones*:

Chocolate Heaven

NICOLE *(18+)* *is on a dinner date with* KRIS. KRIS *is a doctor she recently met in her local hospital where her older sister* LIZ *gave birth.* NICOLE *is a very talkative, energetic woman. One might even describe her as 'hyperactive', a possible symptom of her chocolate addiction.*

NICOLE Well! I never get to twelve o'clock without having at least two or three pieces of chocolate. I can't get past noon without a bite. I'd die without it, I would. Even just thinking about it makes my heart race. I think my favourite is chocolate with a strawberry or raspberry filling, or caramel with a nut, or Turkish delight.

Have you ever tried chocolate mousse? The best is the kind with tens of thousands of air bubbles running through it. Oh, it's to die for ... or chocolate fondue? You melt the chocolate in a bowl, skewer pink and white marshmallows on a cocktail stick and dip into the warm, melted chocolate ...

... ohhhh, bliss!

Chocolate Advent calendars used to frustrate me. All that chocolate! But we were only ever allowed one a day on the run up to Christmas when we were little.

If you put Father Christmas and the Easter Bunny in a boxing ring, my money would have to be on the bunny. That rabbit would knock Santa clean-cut from Christmas to Easter. Am I right? ... Easter eggs! Chocolate eggs to be eaten on Easter Day; so that would almost make eating chocolate a religious or spiritual experience, I'd say. Who thought that one up? Whoever you are, I salute you.

If I ever found myself in Willy Wonka's gigantic, fantastic Chocolate Factory, I'd be Augustus Gloop, the kid the size of a hippopotamus who landed in the chocolate river. I bet you're glad I don't resemble him, huh?! Oh, but listen to me go on, and on. What about you? Tell me a bit about yourself. Just one moment ...

... are you finishing that dessert?

One of the most important features of drama is the fact that it can deal with almost any issue in an intelligent and engaging way. The following two extracts are taken from the Australian play, *What is the Matter with Mary Jane*, written by Wendy Harmer from a story by Sancia Robinson. It tackles the topical but difficult subject of eating disorders and the problems of 'body image'.

Extracts from *What is the Matter with Mary Jane?*

INTRODUCTION

SANCIA is posing in front of the mirror … pouting, pulling her hair back, squeezing her pimples and experimenting with a brand-new cleavage.

Hello, my name is Sancia Robinson, I am 16 years old and I am a size 10 … but it's OK … I know I should be a size 8.

Pleased to meet you … well, I'm not really, because I know you are looking at me thinking: 'Boy, what a fat pig … she could sure lose a few kilos … like 50.'

You're absolutely right … I busted the zip on my shorts this morning … and I've had those shorts for six years! They're my favourite shorts. Now they're just a skin on a bratwurst sausage.

My mum's trying to tell me it's OK … like I'm meant to be growing. Growing into what, Mum? A mutant baked bean?

My whole body is just exploding … I look like an enormous battered saveloy.

Look at my bum. I have a huge bottom … go on … look at it … bean-bag bum … Back of a bus bum. Chubby bum … Excuse me, Miss Robinson, is that your bum or a whopping big bag of Cheezels inside your jeans? 'Never Miss the Seat Sance', they call me.

In fact, there's only one thing in the world more humungous than my bum, and that's my stomach ... have a look at this ... paunchy, pudgy, roly-poly, tubby gut. Spud gut. Old blubber belly. Bag of jelly bean belly.

Have another chocolate biscuit, Sance ... why not? You already look like a Wagon Wheel ... Miss Biscuit Barrel. Miss Monte Carlo. Princess Chocolate Royal. Scone head ... hot buttered scone head ... with two raisins for eyes.

Check me out ... probably the first time you've ever met anyone with Chiko Roll arms, fish fingers and potato-wedge legs. You are what you eat, Sance ... and your body is a bag of junk. I've got the brain of a chicken nugget.

> Two all beef legs,
> no neck
> huge boobs
> fat cheeks.
> All on a sesame seed bum.

I'm sorry ... what did you say your name was again?

*   *   *

In the Mirror

When I am skinny ...

I'll laugh all the time
I'll be very cool
I'll be in the magazines
And look good at the pool.

The sun will be shining
I'll drive a fast car
I'll meet Ronan Keating
I'll be a star.

My eyes will be sparkling
My arms will be brown
My legs will be long
I'll wear a silk gown.

I'll have loads of friends
I'll never be wrong
I'll be healthy and wealthy
wise and strong.

I'll always be kind
I'll always be nice
I'll always be good
I'll only eat rice.

I'll jog every morning
And run every night
I'll be light as a feather
As high as a kite.

I'll only drink water
I'll live on fresh air
I'll float through the heavens
With the moon in my hair.

Oh God ... I think I'm starting to hallucinate.
I must be hungry.
Oh well ... only three hours to tea time.

Dieting is divine ...

Not only is it the way to a fabulous body ... but it's also a miracle cure for everything else that's wrong in your miserable little life.

If you fight with your mum ... you think about lunch.

Hate your brother ... how much do I weigh?

Can't do your maths ... why did I eat that?

Disagree with your teacher ... what did I have for breakfast?

No tears, no pain ... everything under control ... and ... looking good.

As we have seen, drama is capable of dealing with almost any issue experienced by human beings. We complete this section with an extract from a play by the important contemporary Indian playwright Kamala Ramchandani-Naharwar that confronts the problem of AIDS. Here is the opening of *The Big 'A'*:

The Big 'A' by Kamala Ramchandani-Naharwar

ACT I

SCENE 1

GAUTAM I wanted to ask all of you, which of us is not a pretender? That's Aditya over there, victim of The Big 'A' thanks to a transfusion and untested blood.

ADITYA Hey, hey ... wait a minute ... I'm one of the lucky ones ... so far. I'm only HIV positive, I haven't got full-blown AIDS.

GAUTAM And he's a real pretender, plays games, clowns around, thinks life is the Big Apple!

ADITYA And you, Gautam, are the hotline to the next world. After Anand died you couldn't let the poor guy go, could you?

GAUTAM Shut up, Aditya. This is an AIDS ward. Anything can happen.

ADITYA A-a-a-a-ah! [*Mock shivering*] Anything can happen! I'm scared!

GAUTAM Hey, Aditya, what are you scared of? Why are you afraid of me contacting spirits?

ADITYA Heard that? Heard that? Hey, anybody want to chat with their ancestors? Gautam's the guy to contact. He holds a pen in his hand and it talks! Writes down messages from the other world! That's his game.

AYESHA Hi guys! It's me. The friendly neighbourhood ...

ADITYA Spider woman!

GAUTAM Chases all the guys, Hahn? Gave Anand a tough time ...

AYESHA Anand was a hunk! I don't know what he saw in you!

[*LIGHT FOCUS on DOCTOR, his back to the audience, a paper/report in his hand*

ADITYA Hey, what's up with Doc?

GAUTAM Oh, he's got bruises on the brain!

AYESHA He's got all the signs again, he's got to tell someone they've graduated, too!

ADITYA Yup! All 'A's in here! That's what the report card says!

AYESHA Hey, guys, watch ... we got a visitor!

GAUTAM It's Jai Mehta ... a friend of my father ... Good grief! He's come in to meet the Great God Grief!

AYESHA Ya, Doc the Duh who's down in the mouth right now.

GAUTAM Ahuh! You got a soft spot for Doc, Ayesha, it shows!

AYESHA Shut up!

ADITYA [*to AUDIENCE*] Ladies and gentlemen, we ask you all to be pretenders for a while and put yourself in our shoes! Because one day it *can* happen to you.

SCENE 2

JAI and DEEPA enter DOCTOR's space

JAI Hi, Doc! Here I am! Come to donate blood for Gupta's wife!

DOCTOR Jai ... Deepa ...

JAI Come on, let's get it over with fast! Got a meeting ...

DOCTOR Jai, it's not so simple ... I have to tell you something.

JAI Okay, but come on, start taking the blood first, for God's sake, I'm in a hurry, Doc!

DOCTOR Sit down. Both of you.

JAI Why? Is she donating her blood, too? Very good! Come on! Let's get my mother and my two children and make it a family affair!

DOCTOR Jai, listen a minute ...

DEEPA Doctor ... what's wrong ... Look, we know each other well enough ... tell us! It can't be that bad!!

JAI Come on, Doc, just SAY! What's the matter?

GAUTAM And now they all find out they are strangers to themselves and to each other ...

ADITYA Watch the Great God Grief squirm like a worm with his cheery news. What a life! What a bum rap!

DOCTOR We ran some tests ... routine before donating blood ... Jai, you've tested positive ... for AIDS.

[*SILENCE for a few minutes*

JAI For ... AIDS! ... Me!

DEEPA AIDS! AIDS! No!

JAI There's some mistake ...

DOCTOR I wish there were ...

JAI I don't believe you ... I ... don't believe you ...

DOCTOR Here's the report ...

DEEPA Oh God, not ... AIDS ...

[*DOCTOR hands him the report. JAI reads, standing*

JAI [softly] AIDS ...   [*Look at DOCTOR. Puts paper down gently*

GAUTAM Suddenly, he is OLD. He moves old.

ADITYA And now his brain gets turned inside out. [*Imaginary gun to head.*] *Dhachaaak!* *

AYESHA Actually, it hasn't even sunk in.

GAUTAM Stage one: Shock.

JAI How could I get it? ...

AYESHA Stage two: Denial.

JAI I don't believe this!

ADITYA Stage Three: Confident that you'll be the exception who beats it.

JAI Show me that report! I want to see it! I don't have time in my life for AIDS!

GAUTAM Stage Four ...

ADITYA [*sings*] Farewell, world, kiss the sky 'cause that's where you'll go if you've been a good boy!

DEEPA Oh God ...

JAI Do another test.

DOCTOR It'll show the same result.

JAI DO IT!

DEEPA Doctor, please ... there must be some mistake!

DOCTOR We've double-checked.

JAI Why should I believe you?

[*DOCTOR is silent*

You think I can't hear your silence? To you I'm just another case. To me, I'm ME! Understand? Do another test, I said!

DOCTOR I understand.

JAI No, you don't understand! God ... how can you sit ... just ... sit there ...   [*DOCTOR sits silently*

Your tests are wrong! Results wrong!

[*Silence while DOCTOR draws on a pad*

Answer! DAMN YOU!

Got a voice, use it!

You deaf?!

DOCTOR No. I hear too much.

JAI Really?! What d'you do, toss a potato chip, positive, negative, when you do your ... tests?   [*Grabs a piece of paper, shoves it towards*

81

DOCTOR] Here. Write NEGATIVE! Jai Mehta does not have Aids! Write, damn you! I got a life to live! I'm not ready to be kicked out yet!

DOCTOR Okay. Enough. Calm down.   [*Goes to him*

JAI I'm calm. I call this calm. You think this isn't calm? Hahh? How calm do you want me to be? Hahh?

DEEPA What are we going to do? ...

DOCTOR Let's talk about the future.

JAI Future! He talks of a future! HE!!

> [*Suddenly sags. Silent. Empty*

ADITYA He's been zapped! Someone up there dropped a cage over him. Unlike the big 'C', the big 'A's catching. And WHAM! A life is splintered. Broken glass. Everywhere.

DEEPA This isn't true ... It can't be true! Doctor, say it isn't true!

DOCTOR Deepa, you have to face it!

> [*Reaction blank, and she begins to move slowly away, physically and mentally*

JAI Deepa ...

> [*DEEPA nods slowly, blank*

Please ...

> [*JAI moves towards her, she backs slowly away as they talk*

Don't ... back away ...

DEEPA How ... tell me how ... you got this ...

JAI How would I know?

DEEPA You must have some idea ... how?

JAI I've never been unfaithful ... not really ...

DEEPA Then?

> [*Moving away, yet mentally caught now, like to a magnet*

JAI Just ... once.

DEEPA Once.

JAI Yes.

DEEPA Who?

JAI Once in Kolkata ... I met someone ... Just once, Deepa, just once!

DEEPA Once.

JAI Yes. That's all. We were celebrating a business deal. I ... I was drunk, I didn't know what I was doing ... In all these years ... one mistake only, I swear, Deepa ... that's all ...

DEEPA That's all.

JAI Deepa, listen to me ...   [*Moves towards her, she moves away*
Don't turn away.   [*DEEPA says nothing, just keeps moving away*
Don't go ...   [*DEEPA keeps moving*
Deepa, I need you ...   [*DEEPA keeps moving*

GAUTAM Time. A meaningless word for someone under a death sentence. Ha ha! Life ain't easy, it hits where it hurts!

AYESHA And now she'll have to go home. Tell her daughter.

ADITYA Just those few words from the doctor and life dissolves! Nothing is important anymore!

GAUTAM And the word 'time' becomes obsolete.

ADITYA [*holding an imaginary gun to his head*]. *Dischkaooooo!* *

DOCTOR Deepa, there's ... something more ...

DEEPA More.

DOCTOR You'll have to be ... tested ...

DEEPA Oh God, this isn't happening ...

DOCTOR I'm sorry.

DEEPA I don't want to be tested.

JAI Please, Deepa ...

DEEPA I don't want to know.

JAI We have to know about you, Deepa, please ...

DEEPA Don't touch me.

JAI Okay, okay!

DEEPA I don't have it ... I can't have it ... I ... won't have it ...

JAI For ... Maya's sake, Deepa ...

DEEPA Maya ...

JAI Yes ... what will you tell her?

DEEPA The truth.

[*Light fadeout*

---

* *Dhachaaak* and *Dischkaooooo* are onomatopoeic words which imitate the sounds of a pistol being fired.

Intermediate Prose:

This collection of prose pieces continues our theme of storytelling and ranges from what is probably the oldest written story in the world (*The Epic of Gilgamesh*) to contemporary fiction with a strong message for our age (*The Wind in the Pylons*). You are encouraged to use these pieces imaginatively, making your own selection and 'cuts' and use them for drama and group performance as well as for individual speaking.

The Epic of Gilgamesh was written by an unknown author in ancient Mesopotamia (modern Iraq), and was discovered on clay tablets during the nineteenth century. The following extract is the prologue of this wonderful story in a translation by N. K. Sandars:

Prologue of *Gilgamesh King in Uruk*

I will proclaim to the world the deeds of Gilgamesh. This was the man to whom all things were known; this was the king who knew the countries of the world. He was wise, he saw mysteries and knew secret things; he brought us a tale of the days before the flood. He went on a long journey, was weary, worn out with labour, returning he rested, he engraved on a stone the whole story.

When the gods created Gilgamesh they gave him a perfect body. Shamash the glorious sun endowed him with beauty, Adad the god of the storm endowed him with courage, the great gods made his beauty perfect, surpassing all others, terrifying like a great wild bull. Two thirds they made him god and one third man.

In Uruk he built walls, a great rampart, and the temple of blessed Eanna for the god of the firmament Anu, and for Ishtar the goddess of love. Look at it still today: the outer wall where the cornice runs, it shines with the brilliance of copper; and the inner wall, it has no equal. Touch the threshold, it is ancient. Approach Eanna the dwelling of Ishtar, our lady of love and war, the like of which no latter-day king, no man alive can equal. Climb upon the wall of Uruk; walk along it, I say; regard the foundation terrace and examine the masonry: is it not burnt brick and good? The seven sages laid the foundations.

The Patagonian Indians had a ritual for bringing the rain: this description could be used as the basis for a dance-drama as well as for speaking:

Extract from *Ritual for Rain*

It is very hot and everyone is asleep. The Rainmaker, a strangely garbed figure, wakes and stands. He is holding in his hand a bunch of dried twigs. He looks at the sky and sniffs the air. There is no wind. The ground is hot and dry under his feet as he mounts his hill, a mound in the centre of the village. From the top, he gazes round at the sleeping people.

He pauses for a moment and again looks at the sky. He then moves and wakes the sleepers one by one by shaking the dry twigs. They wake gradually and when they are all sitting they begin, conducted by the Rainmaker, to make strange rain and water sounds. This chorus fades to silence and rattles quietly take over. Some of the villagers begin to move and when everyone is wheeling and twisting to the rhythm, the Rainmaker leaps to his hill and signals for stillness and silence. The villagers then begin a low moaning, which increases in speed and volume until everyone is stamping the ground and yelling for rain.

Once more, the Rainmaker signals for silence. A moment later comes the sound of distant thunder. Everyone looks to the hills. It thunders again, nearer this time. The Rainmaker leaps into the air and leads the villagers in a wild, frantic dance. When dark clouds cover the sky the dance slows to a standstill. The Rainmaker cries out to the clouds. The villagers echo his cry. It begins to rain. There is an immense sense of relief. Someone laughs; the laugh is infectious, as everyone enjoys the rain.

The great explorer Marco Polo travelled from Venice in Europe to Cathay (modern China) during the thirteenth century. He left a record of his remarkable adventures in his *Travels of Marco Polo*. In the following extracts he describes the lavish and exotic court life that he discovered:

Extract from *The Travels of Marco Polo*

Chapter 17

Concerning the Twelve Thousand Barons Who Receive Robes of Cloth Garnished with Gems.

Now you must know that the Great Khan has set apart twelve thousand of his men who are distinguished by the name of Keshikten; and on these twelve thousand barons he bestows thirteen changes of raiment, all different from one another. In one set, twelve thousand are all of one colour and there are thirteen different sets of colours. These robes are garnished with gems and pearls and other precious things. And with each change he gives each baron a fine golden girdle of great value.

The Emperor himself has thirteen suits corresponding in colour to those of his barons, though his are grander, richer and costlier. And you may see that what all this costs in incalculable.

Chapter 18

Of the Quantity of Game Sent to the Court During the Winter Months.

At the season when the Great Khan resides in the capital of Cathay, that is during December, January, and February, at which time the cold is excessive, he gives orders for hunting parties to take place in all the areas within forty days' journey of the court.

The governors of districts are then required to send him all sorts of larger game, such as wild boars, stags, fallow deer, roebucks and bears, which are taken in the following manner. All persons owning land in the province go to the places where the animals are found and proceed to encircle and kill them, partly with dogs, but chiefly by shooting them with arrows. Such of them as are intended for his Majesty's use are gutted and then sent on carts, in large quantities, by those who live within thirty stages of the capital. Those who are forty stages away do not, on account of the length of the journey, send the carcasses, but only the skins, some dressed and others raw, to be made use of for the army as his Majesty may judge proper.

Chapter 19

Of Leopard, Lions, and Eagles that the Khan Uses in Hunting.

The Great Khan uses many leopards [*actually cheetah, used from ancient times in hunting*] and lynxes for the purpose of chasing deer. He also uses many lions – larger animals than the Egyptian kind, with beautifully coloured coats striped white, black, and red [*these are evidently tigers*] – to catch boars, wild oxen and asses, bears, stags, roebucks and other beasts that huntsmen prefer. It is a rare sight, when the lion is let loose in pursuit of the animal, to see the savage eagerness and speed with which he overtakes it. His Majesty has them carried in cages on carts, along with a little dog, with which they become familiar. The reason for thus shutting them up is that they would otherwise become so ferocious at the sight of the game that it would be impossible to restrain them. It is necessary to lead them against the wind so that they may not be scented by the game, which would immediately run off.

His Majesty also has eagles that are trained to catch wolves, and such is their size and strength that none, however large, can escape from this talons.

Geoffrey Crump was one of the first teachers of the 'new' subject of speech and drama. In his autobiography, *A Journey in my Head*, he talks about his ideas on teaching and intersperses his thoughts with some amusing memories and stories. Here are two extracts:

Extract from *A Journey in My Head*

Teaching English really means teaching communication, and this is an activity in which most of us are sadly incompetent. It is the purpose for which a language exists, and English people naturally desire to communicate in English. Therefore the old contention that there was no need to learn English because we were English is nonsense – that is the very reason that it is necessary to be fully articulate in one's own native tongue, in order to live in harmony and understanding with one's fellow-countrymen. It has been said, too, that every teacher is a teacher of English, because he teaches in English. That also is nonsense. One has only to listen to many of them teaching to realise that they are doing little service to their native tongue.

One of the earliest and most distinguished teachers of English in this century said that he took his task to be twofold – to teach appreciation and to teach expression. I, too, think that our task is twofold, but I would prefer a different analysis. Appreciation and expression are both, of course, necessary if effective use is to be made of language, but the words suggest something too academic, and insufficiently practical – they smack too much of the text book and the essay. Language is a very everyday business, and it is of universal concern. As I have already said, teaching English means teaching communication, but the task is none the less twofold, because it is necessary to be able both to communicate and to be communicated to. One must not only write and speak efficiently, but read and listen with attention and understanding. This 'silent' aspect of the approach to language has been grossly neglected in the past. It has been described as the 'passive' approach to language as opposed to the active use of writing and speech, but it is not passive – it demands as much activity of mind, even more.

So I resolved that this should be my gospel. The purpose of language in any form – poetry, drama, storytelling, instruction, conversation – is to communicate something to someone else, and that is a two-way process, the four cornerstones of which are Writing, Reading, Speaking and Listening. I saw it as my job to teach these skills, so that my pupils learned to speak and write what they had to say in a way that could be readily understood and was agreeable to read or listen to; also, how to find and choose and read with insight and enjoyment the books they needed and wanted to read, and to cultivate the habit of attentive and intelligent listening.

I must digress for a little to pay my tribute to the memory of Tommy Horder, who was one of my most valued friends. He was a famous doctor, known best for his genius in diagnosis; in his later life, at any rate, when he had decided what was the matter with a patient, he preferred to leave the actual treatment to a specialist or a general practitioner. He was not only a very faithful and generous friend both to me personally and to the Steep Shakespeare Players, but he was a most delightful companion. He had a very engaging and mischievous sense of humour. He was a great gardener, and used to get up early to work in the garden whenever the weather allowed it; he found it possible to do this right up to the end of his life, largely because, at any rate at the time when I knew him, he always rested, and often slept, in the afternoon. He used to say that it was not sleep that was important, but rest; sleep would look after itself if you didn't worry about it. Visitors were apt to think that he was the gardener or even the under-gardener; he loved this, and played up to it as hard as he could. He had a rich hoard of anecdotes, mostly about the medical profession, some of which I must relate. On one occasion, a doctor whom he knew sent a patient to him who had a puzzling skin disease on his arm. 'That looks nasty,' he said; 'but I am not an expert on skin troubles; have you seen a dermatologist?' The patient said that he had, and the dermatologist had asked him if he had had a similar infection before, and he said that he had. 'What did he do about it?' asked Horder. 'Well,' was the reply, 'he said "I'm afraid you've got it again".' He also told me of a rather severe, spinsterish woman who came to consult him. He examined her, and said, 'There are a few questions that I must ask you. Do your bowels work regularly?' 'They'd better,' said the lady. Horder said it was the best answer he had ever had to this question.

Horder was Churchill's doctor. One day, he told me, Churchill came to see him. He said nothing, but paced up and down the consulting room with his hands behind him and a large cigar in his mouth. Horder said nothing either. Presently, Churchill said, 'Horder, I've got gallstones.' Still no reply from Horder. Then Churchill said, 'Don't sit there saying nothing, Horder. Say something!' 'Well,' said Horder, who didn't like his diagnosis to be done for him, 'if you want to know, I was thinking how strange it is that a man of your intelligence should try to teach me my job.' Churchill left abruptly and did not return for some time. The gallstones never materialised.

By all accounts, Jesus was a charismatic storyteller. People were so engrossed by his stories that they sometimes forgot to eat. Here is one of his best-known stories taken from *Luke*, chapter 15, in the Revised Standard Version of the Bible:

Extract from the *Bible*

The Prodigal Son:

There was a man who had two sons. The younger of them said to his father, 'Father, give me the share of the property that will belong to me.' So he divided his property between them. A few days later, the younger son gathered all he had and travelled to a distant country and there he squandered his property in dissolute living. When he had spent everything, a severe famine took place throughout that country and he began to be in need. So he went and hired himself out to one of the citizens of that country, who sent him to his fields to feed the pigs. He would gladly have filled himself with the pods that the pigs were eating; and no one gave him anything. But when he came to himself he said, 'How many of my father's hired hands have bread enough and to spare, but here I am dying of hunger! I will get up and go to my father and I will say to him, 'Father, I have sinned against heaven and before you; I am no longer worthy to be called your son; treat me like one of your hired hands.' So he set off and went to his father. But while he was still far off, his father saw him and was filled with compassion; he ran and put his arms around him and kissed him. Then the son said to him, 'Father, I have sinned against heaven and before you; I am no longer worthy to be called your son.' But the Father said to his slaves, 'Quickly, bring out a robe – the best one – and put it on him; put a ring on his finger and sandals on his feet. And get the fatted calf and kill it, and let us eat and celebrate; for this son of mine was dead and is alive again; he was lost and is found!' And they began to celebrate.

Now his elder son was in the field; and when he came and approached the house, he heard music and dancing. He called one of the slaves and asked what was going on. He replied, 'Your brother has come, and your father has killed the fatted calf, because he has got him back safe and sound.' Then he became angry and refused to go in. His father came out and began to plead with him. But he answered his father, 'Listen! For all these years I have been working like a slave for you, and I have never disobeyed your command; yet you have never given me even a young goat so that I might celebrate with my friends. But when this son of yours came back, who has devoured your property with prostitutes, you killed the fatted calf for him!' Then the father said to him, 'Son, you are always with me, and all that is mine is yours. But we had to celebrate and rejoice, because this brother of yours was dead and has come to life; he was lost and has been found.'

Manon Lescaut, by Abbe Prevost, is one of the greatest love stories ever written. Here is the opening of this eighteenth-century novel in a translation from the French by L. W. Tancock:

Opening of *Manon Lescaut*
I must take you back to the time when I first met the Chevalier des Grieux. It was about six months before I left for Spain. At that time, I lived alone and seldom stirred abroad, but now and again I went on short journeys if my daughter wanted something attended to and I made these as brief as I could. I once had to go to Rouen, where she had asked me to see a case through the Law Courts relating to some land left by my maternal grandfather which I wished to hand over to her. On my way back, I slept the first night at Evreux and reached Passy about five or six leagues further on, in time for dinner. As I came into the little town I was surprised to see all the people rushing out of their houses and gathering in a crowd outside a shabby-looking inn, in front of which two covered waggons were standing. The two waggons had evidently only just arrived, for the horses were still panting and steaming in the shafts. I stopped a moment to find out the cause of the uproar, but I could get no sense out of the gaping crowd, who ignored my questions and kept on fighting their way towards the inn. But just then there appeared in the doorway a soldier, complete with bandolier and musket, and I beckoned him and asked him what all the excitement was about. 'Oh, it's nothing, sir,' he said, 'just a dozen streetwalkers that my friends and I are

taking to Le Havre to be shipped off to America. Some of them aren't bad-looking, either and I suppose that's what these yokels want to see.' I might have left it at that and gone on my way if I had not been pulled up by the cries of an old woman who emerged from the inn wringing her hands and shouting that it was a wicked shame and enough to give anyone the horrors. 'What's the matter?' I asked. 'Oh, come and see, sir! I tell you, it's enough to break your heart!' My curiosity was now thoroughly aroused, and I dismounted, left my horse with my man and forced my way through the crowd. It was certainly a pathetic sight that met my eyes: amongst the twelve women who were chained together by the waist in two rows of six was one whose face and bearing were so out of keeping with her present situation that in any other setting, I would have taken her for a lady of the gentlest birth. She was in abject misery and her clothes were filthy, but all that had so little effect on her beauty that I felt nothing but pity and respect for her. She was trying to turn away as much as the chains would allow, so as to hide her face from us onlookers, and this effort at concealment was so natural that it seemed to come from feelings of modesty. The six guards escorting this party of outcasts were also in the room and I took the one in charge aside and asked him to tell me something about this lovely girl. But he could give me nothing but a few bare facts. 'We picked her up from the hospital on police orders. I don't expect she was put in there for her good behaviour. I have questioned her more than once on the road but can't get a word out of her. But although I haven't got orders to treat her any better than the others, I seem to do little things for her, because she looks a cut above them, somehow. There's a young fellow over there,' he added, 'who might be able to tell you more than I can about what has brought her down to this. He has followed her all the way from Paris. Crying nearly all the time, too. He must be her brother, or else a lover.'

The Wind in the Willows by Kenneth Graham has become one of the most popular stories of all time. It has been made into several plays and has been broadcast on radio. The book's evocation of an idyllic country life on the banks of a river also includes some dark and mystical passages, and it is by no means a simple book to read or speak aloud. Here are the opening moments:

Opening of *The Wind in the Willows*

The Riverbank:

The Mole had been working very hard all the morning, spring cleaning his little home. First with brooms, then with dusters; then on ladders and steps and chairs, with a brush and a pail of whitewash; till he had dust in his throat and eyes, and splashes of whitewash all over his black fur, and an aching back and weary arms. Spring was moving in the air above and in the earth below and around him, penetrating even his dark and lowly little house with its spirit of divine discontent and longing. It was small wonder, then, that he suddenly flung down his brush on the floor, said, 'Bother!' and 'O blow!' and also, 'Hang spring cleaning!' and bolted out of the house without even waiting to put on his coat. Something up above was calling him imperiously, and he made for the steep little tunnel which answered in his case to the gravelled carriage drive owned by animals whose residences are nearer to the sun and air. So he scraped and scratched and scrabbled and scrooged, and then he scrooged again and scrabbled and scratched and scraped, working busily with his little paws and muttering to himself, 'Up we go! Up we go!' till at last, pop! His snout came out into the sunlight and he found himself rolling in the warm grass of a great meadow.

'This is fine!' he said to himself. 'This is better than whitewashing!' The sunshine struck hot on his fur, soft breezes caressed his heated brow, and after the seclusion of the cellarage he had lived in for so long the carol of happy birds fell on his dulled hearing almost like a shout. Jumping off all his four legs at once, in the joy of living and the delight of spring without its cleaning, he pursued his way across the meadow till he reached the hedge on the further side.

'Hold up!' said an elderly rabbit at the gap. 'Sixpence for the privilege of passing by the private road!' He was bowled over in an instant by the impatient and contemptuous Mole, who trotted along the side of the hedge chaffing the other rabbits as they peeped hurriedly from their holes to see what the row was about. 'Onion-sauce! Onion-sauce!' he remarked jeeringly, and was gone before they could think of a thoroughly satisfactory reply. Then they all started grumbling at each other. 'How stupid you are! Why didn't you tell him –' 'Well, why didn't you say –', 'You might have reminded him –' and so on, in the usual way; but, of course, it was then much too late, as is always the case.

It all seemed too good to be true. Hither and thither through the meadows he rambled busily, along the hedgerows, across the copses, finding everywhere birds building, flowers budding, leaves thrusting – everything happy, and progressive, and occupied. And instead of having an uneasy conscience pricking him and whispering 'Whitewash!', he somehow could only feel how jolly it was to be the only idle dog among all these busy citizens. After all, the best part of a holiday is perhaps not so much to be resting yourself, as to see all the other fellows busy working.

Gareth Lovett Jones has used the characters and story of *The Wind in the Willows* as the basis for his powerful warnings about what we are doing to our environment, in **The Wind in the Pylons**. Here is the equivalent section in his book, where Mole has just emerged into the 'world' outside his home:

Opening of *The Wind in the Pylons*

As always, it took the Mole a good half-minute to adjust to the sudden brilliance – although the day was cloudy, so that he did not need to screw up his eyes quite so tightly as if the sun had been out. But even before he could look about him easily, he knew for certain that something was wrong. He sniffed the air, wrinkling up his nose in instant distaste. There was a smell about – several smells, in fact, but one in particular that stood out: acrid, sharp, almost like that of a salt wind blowing off a seaweedy sea, yet seeming to the Mole's sensitive nose not of Nature at all. Straight away, his eyes began to itch. And there was, too, a strange, awesome sound, such as he had never heard before nor could possibly have imagined. It was like a great, continuous exhalation, or rumbling, or combination of the two, in which pulses of whining also grew and then dimmed, grew and then dimmed. Somehow, it seemed far away and close by, all at the same time.

'O, but where *am* I?' he thought to himself, half out loud. 'What can have *happened?*'

As his vision adjusted, so he began to look about him more keenly. And the first thing that struck him, like a hammer blow, was how little there was to see and how utterly, utterly strange what he could see was. Through his own front door, he would come straight up into a grassy meadow, close by a hedge, whose neat rounded shape was always, by late March, dazzlingly patterned over with the tiny white blooms of the blackthorn. There was a great, old oak – not in the hedge, but standing by it – whose arm-like twisted roots had been gnawed and then polished by the oily wool of resting sheep. Yet no such landmarks existed here. Instead, next to him, he found an odd, ugly little short grey post. It had a broad head bearing a door of some kind, embossed with the letters LIOO192PX. It made a low, slow and continuous ticking, like a grandfather clock in the very last moments before it runs down. A few yards behind this object stood a series of broken fragments of hawthorn and elder, growing in a line along a very low bank with wide gaps between them. Far away to the south, in the direction of what ought to have been his everyday entrance, there stood a big, dead tree.

The ground itself was mossed, with blackened stumps of some crop of long ago sticking up from it as if it might once have been ploughland, then abandoned. A line of tall posts made of crude-looking grey-white material ran across it as far as an unmade road. Beyond this, to the Mole's left, stretched a ploughed field so huge that anything that lay beyond it might as well have been in the next county. On this vast space, made toy-like by distance, a strange yellow machine was moving slowly. Behind it, what looked like a white mist swirled out, impossibly, in a row of Catherine-wheeling shapes. The wind was blowing from just this direction.

The Mole hugged himself in anxiety, so startled by the sense of invisible danger all about him that he could not even move back towards the tunnel exit. 'Something terrible – O, *terrible* – has happened here!' he whispered. Yet where *was* "here"? And how had he arrived in it?

'I must go back,' he said, summoning the courage to make a move.

But, just as he was about to take a step he saw a great grey vehicle with immensely fat, ridged tyres bouncing towards him over the rough ground. It was loaded with rolls of what looked like wire, and its engine made a monstrous grating-whining growl of such a violence as he had never before heard nor imagined. Seeing this great beast come on directly at him, or so it seemed, what could any mole have done but turn and run from it? He ran in the direction of the unmade road, and within seconds the thing stood between him and the tunnel exit.

When he reached the track, still in a panic, the Mole hurried on along it. The animals that jumped down from the vehicle – a very rough-looking rabbit and, bizarrely, a couple of stoats – showed not the slightest interest in him, but the Mole was not about to go back and have a chat with them. Instead, puffing nervously, he trotted on towards a distant point where there was at least some hopeful sign of over-hanging vegetation.

'This is not the adventure I wanted!' he whispered. A hundred yards further on, negotiating a large pothole filled with a crumbling black material and pieces of old brick, he said the same thing again, a little louder and rather more petulantly. Here, isolated hawthorns stood a hundred yards apart from one another, trimmed flat across their tops as if at the hand of some lunatic of tidiness. These gradually increased in number until, a quarter of a mile later, the track was lined continuously along one side with blackthorn bushes – as the Mole might have expected – but grown out, and in curiously full bloom. Beyond and above the foam of tiny flowerets, the Mole could also see the rearing grey-green tops of a series of shed-like things, once again inconceivably immense. They were built of deeply ridged materials, wholly unfamiliar to him, and had about them the look and feel of structures thrown up in preparation for a war.

Words were written in towering letters across each of these great null artificial cliff-faces: one, in lemon-yellow, read BRAWSCHE. The one next to it – and it took the Mole nearly a minute to reach it – was made in letters that seemed, astoundingly, to be illuminated from the inside.

This said KANSAS HOMEKARE. Underneath, a flatter, unlit sign read KATCH OUR KRAZY PRICES!!! Beyond this was a very high fence made of some super-heavy-duty criss-cross wire and here, on another sign, were the words UNIVERSAL BREAKDOWN.

'Dear me,' said the Mole. 'O! Dear, dear me! I seem to have come up in Kansas.' He noticed that the sinister breathing-roar, or roaring-breath, ever present in the atmosphere, was much louder here than it had sounded at the tunnel exit. It reached towards him through the leafless branches of a thicket to his right, almost as if it were part of them.

The Mole went on along the track, which by now had a deep screen of hazels and thorns on either side. Under them lay discarded objects: a rusted child's bicycle of an odd design, its frame bent into a sad banana-shape, a rotting mattress in which seedlings had taken root, and ahead, where a bollard bisected the path, a scattering of strange little metal cylinders covered in garishly coloured letters. JILT, read one, ZUPP another, and there, and there, and then again, there were the words POKE-A-POLAR.

There have been many versions of the story of Robin Hood, the outlaw who is supposed to have lived in Sherwood Forrest, robbing the rich to help the poor. In this version, *Maid Marion*, written in the eighteenth century by Thomas Love Peacock, Robin and Marion, disguised as pilgrims, and chased by a baron, have taken refuge in a cottage in the woods:

Extract from *Maid Marion*

'Look ye, master cottager,' said the voice, in an altered tone, 'if you do not let us in willingly, we will break down the door.'

'Ho! Ho!' roared the baron, 'You are become plural, are you, rascals? How many are there of you, thieves? What, I warrant, you thought to rob and murder a poor harmless cottager and his wife, and did not dream of a garrison? You looked for no weapon of opposition but spit, poker, and basting ladle, wielded by unskilful hands: but, rascals, here is short sword, and long cudgel in hands well tried in war, wherewith you shall be drilled into cullenders and beaten into mummy.'

No reply was made, but furious strokes from without resounded upon the door. Robin, Marian, and the baron threw by their pilgrim's attire, and stood in arms on the defensive. They were provided with swords, and the cottager gave them bucklers and helmets, for all Robin's haunts were furnished with secret armouries. But they kept their swords sheathed, and the baron wielded a ponderous spear, which he pointed towards the door ready to run through the first that should enter, and Robin and Marian each held a bow with the arrow drawn to its head and pointed in the same direction. The cottager flourished a strong cudgel (a weapon in the use of which he prided himself on being particularly expert), and the wife seized the spit from the fireplace, and held it as she saw the baron hold his spear. The storm of wind and rain continued to beat on the roof and the casement, and the storm of blows to resound upon the door, which at length gave way with a violent crash, and a cluster of armed men appeared without, seemingly not less than twelve. Behind them rolled the stream, now changed from a gentle and shallow river to a mighty and impetuous torrent, roaring in waves of yellow foam, partially reddened by the light that streamed through the open door, and turning up its convulsed surface in flashes of shifting radiance from restless masses of half-visible shadow. The stepping-stones, by which the intruders must have crossed, were buried under the waters. On the opposite bank, the light fell on the stems and boughs of the rock-rooted oak and ash tossing and swaying in the blast, and sweeping and flashing spray with their leaves.

The instant the door broke, Robin and Marian loosed their arrows. Robin's arrow struck one of the assailants in the juncture of the shoulder, and disabled his right arm: Marian's struck a second in the juncture of the knee, and rendered him unserviceable for the night. The baron's long spear struck on the mailed breastplate of a third, and being stretched to its full extent by the long-armed hero, drove him to the edge of the torrent, and plunged him into its eddies, along which he was whirled down the darkness of the descending stream, calling vainly on his comrades for aid, till his voice was lost in the mingled roar of the waters and the wind. A fourth springing through the door was laid prostrate by the cottager's cudgel: but the wife, being less dexterous than her company, though an Amazon in strength, missed her pass at a fifth, and drove the point of the spit several inches into the right-hand doorpost as she stood close to the left, and thus made a new barrier which the invaders could not pass without dipping under it and submitting their necks to the sword: but one of the assailants, seizing it with gigantic rage, shook it at once from the grasp of its holder and from its lodgement in the post, and at the same time made good the irruption of the rest of his party into the cottage.

Now raged an unequal combat, for the assailants fell two to one on Robin, Marian, and the cottager; while the wife, being deprived of her spit, converted everything that was at hand to a missile, and rained pots, pans, and pipkins on the armed heads of the enemy. The baron raged like a tiger, and the cottager laid about him like a thresher. One of the soldiers struck Robin's sword from his hand and brought him on his knee, when the boy, who had been roused by the tumult and had been peeping through the inner door, leaped forwards in his shirt, picked up the sword and replaced it in Robin's hand, who, instantly springing up, disarmed and wounded one of his antagonists, while the other was laid prostrate under the dint of a brass cauldron launched by the Amazonian dame. Robin now turned to the aid of Marian, who was parrying most dexterously the cuts and slashes of her two assailants, of whom Robin delivered her from one, while a well-applied blow of her sword struck off the helmet of the other, who fell on his knees to beg a boon, and she recognised Sir Ralph Montfaucon. The men who were engaged with the baron and the peasant, seeing their leader subdued, immediately laid down their arms and cried for quarter. The wife brought some strong rope and the baron tied their arms behind them.

'Now, Sir Ralph,' said Marian, 'once more you are at my mercy.'

Another great collector and writer of tales was the Danish Hans Christian Anderson. The following adaptation of his version of *The*

Emperor's New Clothes was included in the most famous of all collections of pieces for performance – *Bell's Standard Elocutionist.* All the great actors of the nineteenth and early twentieth centuries used this book and chose their favourite pieces from it: that is a tradition worth preserving.

Adaptation of *The Emperor's New Clothes*

Many years ago, there lived an Emperor, who was so fond of having new clothes, that he spent all his money upon dress and finery. He had a coat for every hour in the day: and just as in other countries, they say of a king, 'His Majesty is in his council chamber,' they said of him. 'The Emperor is in his dressingroom.'

One day, there came a couple of impostors, who gave themselves out as weavers and pretended that they could weave the most beautiful cloth imaginable. Not only were the colours and pattern of remarkable beauty, but the clothes made of the material, possessed the wonderful quality of being invisible to the eyes of such persons as were either not fit for the office they held, or irremediably stupid.

Those would, indeed, be valuable clothes, thought the Emperor; for, when I put them on, I should be able to find out which men are unfit for their offices and to distinguish the wise from the stupid ones. I must have some of this stuff woven for me directly! – And he gave the two impostors a handsome sum to begin their work with.

They then put up two looms: they asked for the finest silk, and the most splendid gold thread (all of which they put into their pockets), and pretended to be working – working, at the empty looms.

'I should like to know how they are getting on,' thought the Emperor. Yet he felt some misgivings, when he recollected that stupid persons, or such as were unfit for their office, could not see the material. 'Ah! I will send my worthy Prime Minister; he has a great deal of good sense, and nobody is more fit for his office than he.'

The good old Minister accordingly went into the room where the two impostors sat, working at the empty looms. 'Eh! Mercy on us! I can see nothing at all.' But he took care not to say so. The two impostors asked if he did not think the pattern very pretty, and the colours extremely beautiful? 'T-t-t! Can I be so stupid after all? I never thought myself so, and I must not let any one know it! Can I be unfit for my office? ... Oh! It is most elegant, most lovely,' answered the Minister, staring through his spectacles; 'both the pattern, and the colours. I shall be sure to tell the Emperor how pleased I am with the stuff.'

'We are delighted to hear you say so.' And the weavers got more money, more silk, and more gold. They put it all into their pockets as before and kept working, working, working, at the empty looms.

Every visitor spoke of the splendid stuff that was being woven. The Emperor had now a mind to see it himself; so he went, with his retinue, into the room where the two cunning impostors were working away without either warp or woof.

'Is it not magnificent:' And they pointed to the empty loom.

'Why, how's this?' thought the Emperor. 'I can see nothing whatever! This is quite alarming! Can I be stupid? Am I not fit to be Emperor? That would be the most shocking thing that could happen to me! ... Oh, it's very pretty!' cried he; 'it has our most gracious approval!' And he nodded condescendingly, as he gazed at the empty loom – for he would not own that he saw nothing.

'Oh! Ah! It's very pretty!' repeated all his retinue, and they advised him to put on the beautiful new clothes on the day of the public procession. The words, "Elegant!", "Splendid!", "Magnificent!" were bandied about from mouth to mouth; and the Emperor conferred on the two impostors the title of "Weavers to the Imperial Court".

The two impostors sat up the whole of the night preceding the day on which the procession was to take place, and had lit up more than sixteen tapers. People could see them busy at work, finishing the Emperor's new clothes. They imitated the action of taking the stuff off the loom; then they cut it out in the air with large scissors, and proceeded to sew the garments, without either needles or thread, till, at length, they said, 'The clothes are now ready!'

The Emperor then came in, accompanied by the principal Lords of his Court: when the two Imperial weavers, each raising his arms, advanced: 'Sire, here are the trunk-hose, here is the vest, here is the mantle. The tissue is as light as a cobweb, and one might fancy one had nothing on; but that is just its greatest beauty.'

'So it is,' said the courtiers; though they could see nothing, as nothing was there to be seen.

'Will your Imperial Majesty be graciously pleased to take off your clothes?' said the impostors, 'and we will dress you in the new ones, before this large glass.'

The Emperor accordingly took off all his clothes; and, as they pretended to dress him in the new garments, his Majesty turned and twisted himself round, before the looking-glass.

'How capitally the clothes fit!' said all present. 'What a beautiful pattern!' 'What vivid colours!' 'What costly attire!'

'My liege, they are waiting outside with the canopy that is to be carried over your Majesty's head in the procession,' cried the Master of the Ceremonies.

'Ah! I am quite ready, as you may perceive,' answered the Emperor. 'My dress fits nicely – does it not,' added he, turning once more to the glass, as if he were examining its beauties most minutely.

The Lords of the Bed-chamber, who were to bear the train, pretended to pick it up from the floor, with both hands; for they did not venture to show that they saw nothing.

The Emperor then went forth; while his attendants exclaimed:

'Dear me! How incomparably beautiful are the Emperor's new clothes! What a fine train he has, and how well it is cut!' No one, in short, would let his neighbour think that he saw nothing; for it would have been like declaring himself unfit for his office, whatever that might be, or, at best, extremely stupid. None of the Emperor's clothes had ever met with such universal approbation as these.

'But he has got nothing on!' cried at length one little child.

'Only listen to that innocent creature!' said the father; and the child's remark was whispered from one to the other, as a piece of laughable simplicity.

'But he has got nothing on!' cried at length the whole crowd.

This startled the Emperor, for he had an inkling that they were in the right; but he thought: 'I must, nevertheless, face it out till the end. Go on with the procession!'

And the lords-in-waiting went on, marching as stiffly as ever and carrying the train – which did not exist.

There are many examples in fact and fiction of young people discovering their love of drama and performance by presenting plays and entertainments in their own homes. The next example is of what is probably the best known: a description of Christmas in the North American home of the *Little Women* – Jo, Beth, Amy and Meg, in Louisa M. Alcott's book of the same name:

Extract from *Little Women*

On Christmas night, a dozen girls piled onto the bed, which was the dress circle, and sat before the blue and yellow chintz curtains in a most flattering state of expectancy. There was a good deal of rustling and whispering behind the curtain, and, presently, a bell sounded, the curtains flew apart and the 'Operatic Tragedy' began.

'A gloomy wood', according to the one playbill, was represented by a few shrubs in pots, a green baize on the floor, and a cave in the distance. This cave was made with a clothes horse for a roof, bureaux for walls; and in it was a small furnace in full blast, with a black post on it, and an old witch bending over it. A moment was allowed for the first thrill to subside; then Hugo, the villain, stalked in with a clanking sword at his side, a slouched hat, black beard, mysterious cloak, and the boots. After pacing to and fro in much agitation, he struck his forehead, and burst out in a wild strain, singing of his hatred of Roderigo, his love for Zara, and his pleasing resolution to kill the one and win the other. The audience applauded the moment he paused for breath, and bowing with the air of one accustomed to public praise, he ordered Hagar to come forth with a commanding, 'What ho! Minion I need thee!'

Out came Meg, with grey horse hair hanging about her face, a red and black robe, a staff, and cabalistic signs upon her cloak. Hugo demanded a potion to make Zara adore him, and one to destroy Roderigo. Hagar, in a fine dramatic melody, promised both and proceeded to call up the spirit who would bring the love philtre:

"Hither, hither, from thy home,
Airy sprite, I bid thee come!
Born of roses, fed on dew,
Charms and potions canst thou brew?
Bring me here, with elfin speed,
The fragrant philtre which I need;
Make it sweet, and swift and strong;
Spirit, answer now my song!"

A soft strain of music sounded and then at the back of the cave appeared a little figure in cloudy white, with glittering wings, golden hair and a garland of roses on its head. Waving a wand, it sung:

"Hither I come
From my airy home,
Afar in the silver moon;
Take the magic spell,
Oh, use it well!
Or its power will vanish soon."

And dropping a small gilded bottle at the witch's feet, the spirit vanished. Another chant from Hagar produced another apparition – not a lovely one, for, with a bang, an ugly black imp appeared, and having croaked a reply, tossed a dark bottle at Hugo and disappeared with a mocking laugh. Having warbled his thanks, and put the potions in his boots, Hugo departed; and Hagar informed the audience that, as he had killed a few of her friends in times past, she had cursed him, and intended to thwart his plans, and be revenged on him. Then the curtain fell, and the audience reposed and ate candy while discussing the merits of the play.

A good deal of hammering went on before the curtain rose again; but when it became evident what a masterpiece of stage-carpentering had been got up, no one murmured at the delay. It was truly superb! A tower rose to the ceiling; halfway up appeared a window with a lamp burning at it, and behind the white curtain appeared Zara in a lovely blue-and-silver dress, waiting for Roderigo. He came, in gorgeous array, with plumed cap, red cloak, chestnut lovelocks, a guitar, and the boots, of course.

Kneeling at the foot of the tower, he sung a serenade in melting tones. Zara replied, and after musical dialogue, consented to fly. Then came the grand effect of the play. Roderigo produced a rope ladder with five steps to it, threw up one end, and invited Zara to descend. Timidly, she crept from her lattice, put her hand on Roderigo's shoulder, and was about to leap gracefully down, when, 'alas, alas for Zara!' she forgot her train – it caught in the window; the tower tottered, leaned forward, fell with a crash, and buried the unhappy lovers in the ruins!

A universal shriek arose as the russet boots waved wildly from the wreck, and a golden head emerged, exclaiming, 'I told you so! I told you so!' With wonderful presence of mind, Don Pedro, the cruel sire, rushed in and dragged out his daughter with a hasty aside –

'Don't laugh; act as if it was all right!' and ordering Roderigo up, banished him from the kingdom with wrath and scorn. Though decidedly shaken by the fall of the tower upon him, Roderigo defied the old gentleman, and refused to stir. This dauntless example fired Zara; she also defied her sire, and he ordered them both to the deepest dungeons of the castle. A stout little retainer came in with chains, and led them away, looking very much frightened, and evidently forgetting the speech he ought to have made.

Act three was the castle hall; and here Hagar appeared, having come to free the lovers and finish Hugo. She hears him coming, and hides; sees him put the potions into two cups of wine, and bid the timid little servant, 'Bear them to the captives in their cells, and tell them I shall come anon.' The servant takes Hugo aside to tell him something, and Hagar changes the cups for two others which are harmless. Ferdinando, the "minion", carries them away, and Hagar puts back the cup which holds the poison meant for Roderigo. Hugo, getting thirsty after a long warble, drinks it, loses his wits and after a good deal of clutching and stamping, falls flat and dies.

This was a truly thrilling scene; though some persons might have thought that the sudden tumbling down of a quantity of long hair rather marred the effect of the villain's death.

Intermediate Poetry:

The poems in this section are all by living or modern writers and are chosen to illustrate that poetry has real significance in the contemporary world, yet does not always have to be solemn to be serious. Even when the poem is not a narrative poem, there is still a personal story behind it that needs communicating to an audience.

There is a challenge in this anonymous poem for you to see how many ways there are to say 'I Dunno'.

I Dunno (Anon.)

I sometimes think I'd rather crow
And be a rooster than to roost
And be a crow. But I dunno.

A rooster he can roost also,
Which don't seem fair when crows can't crow
Which may help some. Still I dunno.

Crows should be glad of one thing though;
Nobody thinks of eating crow,
While roosters they are good enough
For anyone unless they're tough.

There's lots of tough old roosters though,
and anyway a crow can't crow,

So mebbe roosters stand more show.
It looks that way. But I dunno.

Paddy Hughes writes about almost every aspect of our modern world and also creates scripts, sometimes in verse, for television and movies. You will find more about him and another of his poems in the advanced selection.

North Sea Oil by **Paddy Hughes**

North
in a codless sea
sheaves of steel straw
tied at the top
with nests of glittering deck
suck blackly
drink history

Sea
in a ruthless night
lines of gigantic horses
foam from the lip
down flanks of a million mirrors
aflare with gold
muck and brass

Oil
in an empty sea
husks of rusty rig
flaked by frost
skeletons of wind singing
a grey dirge
the urge gone

The Wetlands by **Paddy Hughes**

More and more of the land
is stealing a second-hand sky
and hiding under reproduction clouds.

More and more of my boots
dive into unplumbed oceans
between tousled islands of mud.

The night has raised sea levels,
Ice
caps plotting from afar,
glaciers stealthily melting the weather.

My labrador splashes with relish;
she's descended from a seal.
I have a hole in my boot for tepid squelching.

The cycle track's been drowned
by the golf course and has stopped
wriggling. The deer need raincoats.

Parts of the Park
are almost joined to the Amazon.

Henry Normal combines poetry writing with a career in theatre, TV and movies. Here are a few of his wonderfully observant and wry poems:

Life by Mail Order by **Henry Normal**

There's a change of style
within your magazine
you sit there by his side
a clean-cut guy
at ease he smiles
lightweight suit
well-groomed hair
depth in character
a good all-rounder
drinks in the bank
at ease he smiles
at ease he smiles
within your magazine

There's a change of style
within your magazine
you stand by the blind
you turn and smile
looking good
matching pine
hanging plants
home baking
home making
freezer full of food
drapes to match the sofa

credit at your fingertips
looking good
feeling good
within your magazine

Socks Appeal by **Henry Normal**

Some people like leather socks
or fish-net socks
glittery or spangly socks
Some people don't like socks at all
some people wear socks out of duty
or convention
Some people wear socks for show
me
I like warm socks
soft to the touch
that cushion you from the coldest of floors
and hold you gently
spreading a glow through your whole body
You can feel at home
and secure anywhere in warm socks
and
I get the feeling
nothing bad could
ever happen in the warmest of socks
the sort
you never want to take off

Third World War Poems by **Henry Normal**

1. To show how easy it is for a mistake to happen
  Hickory Dickory Dock
  The mouse ran up the clock
  the clock struck one
  causing a pre-emptive strike escalating
  into all out nuclear attack
  Hickory Dickory Dock

2. About weapons falling into the wrong hands
Mary had a little lamb
She also had a thermo nuclear device
the Armageddon activity set
new from Fisher Price

3. Class comment
Humpty Dumpty sat on a wall
Humpty Dumpty had a great fall
All the King's horses and all the King's men
were safely tucked away in underground bunkers

4. About the effects of nuclear fallout
Mary Mary quite contrary
how does your garden grow?
It doesn't.

5. In a similar vein
I had a little pear tree
and nothing would it bear

Geoffrey Crump, about whom you can learn much more in the prose section, was not only a teacher and performer, but also a published poet. The following is one of his lyrical pieces:

Up on the Downs by **Geoffrey Crump**

As I rode up from the valley below
She sat on a gate in the sunset glow,
Almost unreal in that golden light –
A lovely and disturbing sight.

She made no move, but it seemed absurd
To pass her by without a word,
So I stopped, and said in a friendly way
'Hasn't it been a lovely day?'
But she, it seemed, had nothing to say.

It was an unkind trick of fate
That she should be perched on a five-barred gate
While I sat grandly aloft on a horse;
It must have embarrassed her, of course.
She didn't smile, but she stared at me,
and her dark eyes held mine steadily.
'Well, well' I thought: 'you never know;
She's certainly looking at me as though –'
But I lost my nerve. I let it go.

I rode off slowly along the track,
Firmly determined to look back;
And before very long she was lost to sight.

Was I afraid
Of the silent maid
Who sat and gazed at me from that gate?

Alas, I know now, know too late,
That everything would have been all right.

The next poem comes from Scotland and focuses on a mode of communication that can have many forms and meanings: a kiss. Some very short poems contain complex ideas and demand very skilled speaking:

A Kiss by **Fredrica Rose**

A kiss can be as warm and loving as a summer's day.
A kiss can mean goodbye, heartache and tears.
Or it can be bestowed, ice-cold and false,
On either cheek, in pompous ceremony.
A kiss can pout so sweetly from a baby's mouth,
Or linger in a letter, fragrance filled.
And then the lover's kiss, hungry and passion led,
Or wafted, finger to the lips, like thistledown.
What is a kiss? – Essence of life itself, joyous or bittersweet.

Gillian Bickley writes from her experience of life in modern Hong Kong, where the speaking of poetry is a very popular art form:

Exit by **Gillian Bickley**

Yesterday I saw a butterfly, slightly disturbed,
but purposeful, the possibility of hysteria
only
a possibility
contradicting my inward descent into the subway
flying on a route that would take it out
as I hurried down steps that led me in.
Today, I saw a caterpillar, small and thin
possibly the same species.
Perhaps there will be a generation of butterflies
teaching us the way out.

1970–1997

Survival by **Gillian Bickley**

Thank you trees for being there, for staying
when many of the friends you knew –
birds and butterflies – have gone;
for flourishing, even; growing old
where concrete buildings
are constantly knocked down.
How brave you are to survive
in a place where the air is foul
and the noise unnatural;
you who should normally expect
to stabilise your roots
in humid humming forests
alive with the smells of
animal and vegetable life
(not the smells of mineral death, as here).
It is good to look down a street
and, amazed, to see you there
solid and green and cool, uncompromised
by the advertising posters on your boles;
a promise
that, since there was a past
there may quite possibly be a future too

1970–1997

We have already met the poetry of Geoffrey Crump, who was one of the founders of the Society of Teachers of Speech and Drama. This international organisation encourages young people to write poetry through its competitions and we are pleased to be including some of the winning poems from a recent competition:

Hello ... by **Nadia El-Sayed**

As I stand alone in a place
Where no one knows my name,
I remember you and what you said
Many long years ago.

You told me that here
You would for an eternity be,
That as I believe in you
I'll never be alone.

The weeks went by and I watched you
Slowly grow weak and frail,
I swear I never left your side
Though you gradually left mine.

I love you my dear –
Nothing can ever change that,
But this is the final time I'll come and visit you here.

Yet here I am at the very same place
We visited together so many past years past,
As I want you to know that still
And always I will believe in you.

Flooding by Conor Hacon

A black veil screens light,
Harsh rains are whipped upon heads.
Dark horses of the high seas overwhelm defences,
Overthrowing our power as top predator.

Unsuspecting properties looted, of treasure,
Leaving only the foul stench of decline.
No emotions, no apology, no regret.
It's prize grand, its authority recognised.

The following intriguing poem is by one of Australia's most inventive poets – C. J. Dennis:

The Ant Explorer by C. J. Dennis

Once a little sugar ant made up his mind to roam –
To fare away far away, far away from home.
He had eaten all his breakfast, and he had his Ma's consent
To see what he could chance to see and here's the way he went –
Up and down a fern front, round and round a stone,
Down a gloomy gully where he loathed to be alone,
Up a mighty mountain range, seven inches high
Through the fearful forest grass that nearly hid the sky,
Out along a bracken bridge, bending in the moss,
Till he reached a dreadful desert that was feet and feet across.
'Twas a dry, deserted desert, and a trackless land to tread;
He wished that he was home again and tucked-up tight in bed
His little legs were wobbly, his strength was nearly spent,
And so he turned around again and here's the way he went –
Back away from desert lands feet and feet across,
Back along the bracken bridge bending in the moss,

116

Through the fearful forest grass, shutting out the sky,
Up a mighty mountain range seven inches high,
Down a gloomy gully, where he loathed to be alone,
Up and down a fern front and round and round a stone,
A dreary ant, a weary ant, resolved no more to roam,
He staggered up the garden path and popped back home.

The next two poems deal with lighthouses: W. W. Gibson's *Flannan Isle* provides a gripping mystery and was written in the early twentieth century by one of a group of poets who were particularly concerned with the speaking of poetry. This poem can also make an intriguing play:

Flannan Isle by W. W. Gibson

'Though three men dwell on Flannan Isle
To keep the lamp alight,
As we steered under the lee, we caught
No glimmer through the night!'

A passing ship at dawn had brought
The news; and quickly we set sail,
To find out what strange thing might ail
The keepers of the deep-sea light.

The winter day broke blue and bright,
With glancing sun and glancing spray,
While o'er the swell our boat made way,
As gallant as a gull in flight.

But, as we neared the lonely Isle;
And looked up at the naked height;
And saw the lighthouse towering white,
With blinded lantern, that all night

Had never shot a spark
Of comfort through the dark,
So ghostly in the cold sunlight
It seem'd, that we were struck the while
With wonder all too dread for words.

And, as into the tiny creek
We stole beneath the hanging crag,
We saw three queer, black, ugly birds –
Too big, by far, in my belief,
For guillemot or shag –
Like seamen sitting bolt upright
Upon a half-tide reef:
But, as we near'd they plunged from sight,
Without a sound, or spurt of white.

And still too 'mazed to speak,
We landed; and made fast the boat;
And climb'd the track in single file,
Each wishing he were safe afloat,
On any sea, however far,
So it be far from Flannan Isle:
And still we seemed to climb, and climb,
As though we'd lost all count of time,
And so must climb for everyone.
Yet, all too soon, we reached the door –
The black, sun-blister'd lighthouse door.
That gaped for us ajar.

As, on the threshold, for a spell,
We paused, we seemed to breathe the smell
Of limewash and of tar,
Familiar as our daily breath,
As though 'twere some strange scent of death:

And so, yet wondering, side by side,
We stood a moment, still tongue-tied:
And each with black foreboding eyed
The door, ere we should fling it wide,
To leave the sunlight for the gloom:
Till, plucking courage up, at last,
Hard on each other's heels we pass'd,
Into the living room.

Yet, as we crowded through the door,
We only saw a table, spread
For dinner, meat and cheese and bread;
But, all untouch'd; and no one there:
As though, when they sat down to eat,
Ere they could even taste,
Alarm had come; and they in haste
Had risen and left the bread and meat:
For at the table-head a chair
Lay tumbled on the floor.

We listen'd; but we only heard
The feeble chirping of a bird
That starved upon its perch:
And, listening still, without a word,
We set about our hopeless search.

We hunted high, we hunted low;
And soon ransack'd the empty house;
Then o'er the Island, to and fro,
We ranged, to listen and to look
In every cranny, cleft or nook
That might have hid a bird or mouse:
But, though we search'd from shore to shore,

We found no sign in any place:
And soon again stood face to face
Before the gaping door:
And stole into the room once more
As frighten'd children steal.

Aye: though we hunted high and low,
And hunted everywhere,
Of the three men's fate we found no trace
Of any kind in any place,
But a door ajar, and an untouch'd meal,
And an overtoppled chair.

And as we listened in the gloom
Of that forsaken living room –
A chill clutch on our breath –
We thought how ill chance came to all
Who kept the Flannan Light:
And how the rock had been the death
Of many a likely lad:
How six had come to a sudden end,
And three had gone stark mad:
And one whom we'd all known as friend
Had leapt from the lantern one still night,
And fallen dead by thc lighthouse wall:
And long we thought
On the three we sought,
And of what might yet befall.

Like curs a glance has brought to heel,
We listen'd, flinching there:
And look'd, and look'd, on the untouch'd meal,
And the overtoppled chair.

We seemed to stand for an endless while,
Though still no word was said,
Three men alive on Flannan Isle,
Who thought on three men dead.

The Irish poet Dermot Bolger provides an equally haunting picture of a deserted lighthouse:

***Keepers of the Baily Light* by Dermot Bolger** (for Bill Long)

The keepers are gone, this watchroom deserted.
Just a few books left in the small wall cabinet
Marked *Carnegie Libraries for Lighthouse Service.*

A crime paperback, Lloyd's Register of Ships,
Her Majesty's Sea Captain's Medical Guide
And a 1955 Radio Signals Admiralty List.

Four times a minute a three-quarter second flash
Ranges across sandbanks, drifting nets and unlit buoys
To where twice each sixteen seconds the Kisk replies.

A fly settles on a daybook crammed with letters,
Berating P. Cunningham in 1959 for taking a taxi
From Crookhaven to Cork when a bus was cheaper,

Cutting L. J. Kennedy's 1966 hackney fare in half,
Requesting personnel to wear white-topped caps
And S. O'Sullivan to vaccinate against small pox.

These folded letters, the brisk officious terms
Are the sole remnants of the confraternity of men
Who struggled with solitude, gales and regulations.

But microscopic clues remain in their fingerprints
That annotate the margins of curt communiqués
Like the notes bored scribes left on medieval gospels.

Thoughts pinned like moths in each crinkled fold:
'*I crave wood to carve with, I crave my children.*'
'*I only feel safe here beyond the world's reach.*'

'*Christ, I can't bear another watch on my own,*
Lights of distant ships in this prison of silence,
I want to scream and tear these walls down.'

'*The doctors and their tests, maybe they are wrong.*'
'*My son is drinking hard and I can't stop him,*
I could not be there and now the chance is gone.'

The trapped fly takes flight, its buzzing magnified,
In that curved room where men played solitaire,
By the vast unlit windows bereft of watching eyes.

We conclude this section with two typical pieces from the collection of poems entitled *Mischief City* by the Canadian poet Tim Wynne-Jones:

Talking by Tim Wynne-Jones
We're driving down the highway
And I'm hanging out the door –
But Mom and Dad are talking.
They do a lot of talking.
And when Mom and Dad are talking,
They don't see me anymore.

I'm lying on the table
About to eat my chair!
But Mom and Dad are talking.
They do a lot of talking.
And when Mom and Dad are talking,
They don't even know I'm there.

Hey, Mom! I shout. Hey, Father!
I'm leaving on the bus!
But Mom and Dad are talking.
They do a lot of talking.
And when Mom and Dad are talking,
It's no use to make a fuss.

So I pack my bag with cookies,
Put my sneakers on my feet.
'Cause Mom and Dad are talking.
They do a lot of talking.
And when Mom and Dad are talking,
That's when I hit the street.

What is it, dear? calls Mommy.
What is it, dear? calls Pop.
They've finally finished talking.
They've had enough of talking.
Yes, now they've finished talking,
But it's too late – I forgot!

I Wasn't Angry When I Thought About Maxine by Tim Wynne-Jones

It was raining out on the street
The cars drove by splitter-splat.
Mom was painting the spare bedroom blue,
Baby was taking her nap.
Dad was away on a trip that day,
Due back on the five-fifteen.
And that's when I made my very best friend,
That's when I drew Maxine.

Sometimes when you draw, your pencil knows
Exactly what to do.
Both eyes came out the very same size,
And just the right shade of blue.
The ears and the nose and the mouth that I chose,
Were all the best features to pick.
I made her hair green for the heck of it,
But I made it shiny and thick.
And I gave her a dress that was striped like a rainbow,
And shoes that were ultramarine.
And when it was done, I knew that was the one –
The very best ever – Maxine.

I took down all of the pictures I had
On my bulletin board that day.
I picked purple push-pins
(To match her gloves)
And I put all the others away.
The sun came out as I tidied my desk,
I tidied it, neat and clean.
Then Baby woke up and Mom brought her in
And that's when I showed them Maxine.

Sometimes when you draw, your pencil knows
Exactly what to do.
I counted the fingers, made sure there were ten,
And I counted the hands, there were two.
She had elbows and knees – I have trouble with knees –
But this time I got them on right.
I even remembered to give her some socks,
The socks that I gave her were white.
And I gave her a dress that was striped like a rainbow,
And shoes that were ultramarine.
Baby went wild, Mom squeezed me and smiled,
They loved her, like I did, Maxine.

THE ADVANCED COLLECTION

The attainments expected from audition candidates and those entering examinations at grades 6–8 are very considerable, and range from a growing sense of competence and ownership to self-motivated and designed learning. At this level, too, there must be an awareness of form, genre and the significant periods and contexts of writing, both in English and in what is now translated into English. Accordingly, this section shows some elements of historical development for all forms of writing and provides suitable material for the specific requirements of examinations in terms of period and style.

What I hope to demonstrate in this section is that the personal narrative, whether it be in a prose passage, poem or play, remains a potent means of saying something significant about the world and the problems of living within it. The material here requires depth of thought, involvement with complex emotions and engagement with sophisticated argument. Once that level of understanding is realised in performance, it will draw on advanced physical, vocal and imaginative skills and demand extensive research into original context.

I hope that, like generations of students and performers before them, the teachers and candidates who explore this material will find that the quality of the ideas and writing will challenge and extend their perceptions and abilities.

Drama from Various Periods of Theatre History:

Ancient Greece:

There are now many translations and adaptations that give us access to the great dramas of Aeschylus, Euripides, Sophocles or Aristophanes. Modern versions include those by Tony Harrison, the Caribbean poet Derek Walcott, the Irish poet Seamus Heaney and the Australian feminist writer Germaine Greer, as well as those by Michael James Gould, who has set himself the task of translating and publishing all the finest plays from Ancient Greece.

Gilbert Murray, who provided the role model for the Professor of Greek, Adolphus Cusins, in G. B. Shaw's play *Major Barbara*, made the first genuinely workable English translations of Greek plays between 1904 and 1908. The following is a speech from his translation of *Alcestis* by Euripides:

Extract from *Alcestis* by Euripides

ALCESTIS *has agreed to go to death in the Underworld in place of her husband* ADMETUS. *She bids farewell to* ADMETUS *and their* CHILDREN.

ALCESTIS Admetus, seeing what way my fortunes lie,
    I fain would speak with thee before I die.
    I have set thee before all things; yea, mine own
    Life beside thine was naught. For this alone
    I die ... Dear Lord, I never need have died.
    I might have lived to wed some prince of pride,
    Dwell in a king's house ... Nay, how could I, torn
    From thee, live on, I and my babes forlorn?
    I have given to thee my youth – not more nor less,
    But all – though I was full of happiness.
    Thy father and mother both – 'tis strange to tell –
    Had failed thee, though for them the deed was well,
    The years were ripe, to die and save their son,
    The one child of the house: for hope was none,
    If thou shouldst pass away, of other heirs.

So thou and I had lived through the long years,
Both. Thou hadst not lain sobbing here alone
For a dead wife and orphan babes ... 'Tis done
Now, and some God hath wrought out all his will.
  Howbeit I now will ask thee to fulfil
One great return-gift – not so great withal
As I have given, for life is more than all;
But just and due, as thine own heart will tell
For thou hast loved our little ones as well
As I have ... Keep them to be masters here
In my old house; and bring no stepmother
Upon them. She might hate them. She might be
Some baser woman, not a queen like me,
And strike them with her hand. For mercy, spare
Our little ones that wrong. It is my prayer ...
They come into a house: they are all strife
And hate to any child of the dead wife ...
Better a serpent than a stepmother!
  A boy is safe. He has his father there
To guard him. But a little girl! [*Taking the
Little Girl to her*] What good
And gentle care will guide thy maidenhood?
What woman wilt thou find at father's side?
One evil word from her, just when the tide
Of youth is full, would wreck thy hope of love.
And no more mother near, to stand above
Thy marriage-bed, nor comfort thee pain-tossed
In travail, when one needs a mother most!
Seeing I must die ... 'Tis here, across my way,
Not for the morrow, not for the third day,
But now – Death, and to lie with things that were.
  Farewell. God keep you happy. – Husband dear,
Remember that I failed thee not; and you,
My children, that your mother loved you true.

In Michael James Gould's very recent translation of *Medea,* by Euripides of Athens, we find this wonderful opening speech by the elderly nurse who sets the scene and provides the context for the rest of the play:

Extract from *Medea* by Euripides

Morning.

> *The CHILDREN's elderly NURSE enters from MEDEA's house*

NURSE Through the dark grey razor-sharp rocks
How I wish the ship of Argo
Never flew to far off Colchis,
And the cut pines hadn't fallen
On the wooded slopes of Pelion,
Out of which the oars were fashioned
For the hands of men the finest,
Who went off to fetch the gold fleece
At the order of King Pelias.

Had this voyage never happened,
Poor Medea, who's my mistress,
Had not sailed to Iolcus Castle,
Heart on fire with love for Jason,
Where she wouldn't have persuaded
Pelias' girls to kill their father,
Nor be living here in Corinth
With her husband and her children,
Where her loyalty to Jason
Was so pleasing to its freemen,
Since a woman's safest conduct
Is agreement with her husband.

Closest friendships turn to hatred.
Deepest love is disregarded.
Jason's made a royal marriage
With the daughter of King Creon,
Who's the ruler of this country.

Poor Medea, scorned and slighted,
Shouts aloud his wedding pledges
And the solemn oaths he uttered;
Calls the gods to be her witness
How he's broken every promise.
Giving in to her emotions,
She lies fasting, she lies weeping.
All her day is passed in teardrops,
Since she learnt of her betrayal.

Eyes and face are firmly downcast.
Hears no more the consolation
Any friends may try to offer
Than a rock in choppy waters,
Saving when she twists her white neck
To bewail her dear old father,
Home and country she surrendered
For the man with whom she came here:
Since he's treated her so badly,
She has learnt through this disaster
Just how vital is your homeland.

Now alas she hates her children,
Has no pleasure when she sees them.
I'm afraid of what she's planning,
For she has a dreadful temper,
Cannot bear to suffer wrongly.

As I know her I'm suspecting
She will stab right through her stomach,
Having sneaked into the chamber,
Where the bridal bed is laid out,
Kill the king and then the bridegroom,
Taking chances on the outcome.
For she is a holy terror:
Take her on in any contest,
You'd be most hard put to beat her.

Further Suggestions:

Investigate plays by Jean Paul Sartre, T. S. Eliot, Eugene O'Neill, Jean Anouilh or Carol Ann Duffy that use themes, techniques and ideas drawn from the Ancient Greek Theatre.

Medieval Drama: (Fourteenth and Fifteenth Century)

Wherever the Christian Church was established in the medieval world, groups or 'cycles' of plays exploring themes and stories from the Bible became popular. We have included God's opening speech from one such cycle and an early example of a soliloquy from the medieval morality play, *Everyman*. You should remember that both the roles of God and of Everyman have been played by women in modern productions of these plays:

Extract from *The Midlands Mysteries*
(An adaptation of the N-Town cycle by Douglas Sugano and Ken Pickering)

   GOD *appears in Heaven, GOOD ANGELS sing*

GOD Now heaven is made for angels' sake
The first day and the first night.   [*As* GOD *commands, the earth,*
                  water, land, trees appear

The second day water I make,
The firmament also, full fair and bright.
The third day I part water from earth;
Tree and every growing thing,
Both herb and flower of sweet smelling,
The third day is made by my working.
Now make I the day that shall be the fourth:

> [*As* GOD *orders, sun, moon, stars,
> Paradise and animals appear*

Sun and moon and stars also,
The fourth day I make in-same.
The fifth day sea creatures and fish that swim and go,
Birds and beasts, both wild and tame.

> [GOD *comes down to Paradise to make*
> ADAM *and* EVE

The sixth day my work I do
And make thee, man, Adam by name.
In earthly paradise withouten woe
I grant thy bidding, unless thou do blame.
Flesh of thy flesh and bone of thy bone,
Adam, here is thy wife and mate.
Both fish and fowl that swim and gon,
To everyone of them a name thou take;
Both tree and fruit, and beasts each one,
Red and white, both blue and black,
Give thou them names by thyself alone,
Herb and grass, both beet and braken,
Thy wife thou give name also.
Look that thee not cease
Your fruit to increase
That there may be press
Me worship for to do.

> [GOD *guides* ADAM *through Paradise*

Now come forth, Adam, to Paradise!
There shalt thou have all manner of thing;

Flesh and fish, and fruit of price,
There shall be plenty at thy bidding.
Here is pepper, peony, and sweet licorice;
Take them all at thy liking,
Apple and pear and gentle rice,
But touch not this tree that is of cunning.
All thing save this for thee is wrought.
Here is all thing that thee should please
All ready make onto thine ease.
Eat not this fruit nor me displease,
For then thou diest, thou 'scapest not!

Now have I made all thing of nought,
Heaven and earth, fowl and beast.
To all thing that my hand hath wrought
I grant mine blessing that ever shall last.
My way to heaven is ready sought,
Of working I will the seventh day rest.
And all my creatures that be about,
My blessing ye have both east and west.
Of working the seventh day ye cease.
And all that cease of labouring here
The seventh day, without a fear,
And worship me in good manner,
They shall in heaven have endless peace.

Adam, go forth and be prince in place,
For to heaven I speed my way.
Thy wits well look thou prize,
And the spirit govern thee as I say.

[*GOD exits to Heaven*

Everyman is one of the great Medieval Morality plays in the English language. In the following incident, the central character Everyman has been told that his life is ending and that he must go on a journey to face his maker. He attempts to persuade various friends and relations to go with him:

Extract from *Everyman*

EVERYMAN O, to whom shall I make my moan
    For to go with me in that heavy journey?
    First Fellowship said he would with me gone;
    His words were very pleasant and gay,
    But afterward he left me alone.
    Then spake I to my kinsmen, all in despair,
    And also they gave me words fair;
    They lacked no fair speaking,
    But all forsook me in the ending.
    Then went I to my Goods, that I loved best,
    In hope to have comfort, but there had I least;
    For my Goods sharply did me tell
    That he bringeth many into hell.
    Then of myself I was ashamed,
    And so I am worthy to be blamed;
    Thus may I well myself hate.
    Of whom shall I now counsel take?
    I think that I shall never speed
    Till that I go to my Good Deed.
    But, alas, she is so weak
    That she can neither go nor speak;
    Yet will I venture on her now.
    My Good Deeds, where be you?

Further Suggestions:
- The Messenger's opening speech from *Everyman*.
- Shepherds' speeches from *The Wakefield Cycle*.
- Nativity scenes from *The York Cycle*.
- Excellent editions of all the major cycles are available with modernised spelling and textual notes.

The Sixteenth Century:

Towards the end of the sixteenth century, London became the most active and concentrated centre of theatre in the world; perhaps this is one of the reasons why, many years later, both Trinity and Guildhall were established there. Hundreds of plays were written to satisfy the huge public demand and the playwright Christopher Marlowe created a form of dramatic verse, later employed by Shakespeare, that transformed forever the nature of stage language in English.

A defining moment in Renaissance drama occurs in Marlowe's *Dr Faustus*, based on an old German story. The protagonist discovers that hell is no longer the burning fire of medieval drama, but right here where *we* make it:

Extract from: *Dr Faustus*, by Christopher Marlowe

FAUSTUS has signed away his soul to Lucifer in exchange for twenty-four years of unlimited pleasure and power. He is able to conjure up MEPHISTOPHILIS to serve him and engages in 'disputations' with him. This chilling duologue is the key moment and could be played by performers of either sex.

MEPH Now, Faustus, what wouldst thou have me do?
FAUST I charge thee wait upon me whilst I live,
　　　 To do whatever Faustus shall command,
　　　 Be it to make the moon drop from her sphere,
　　　 Or the ocean to overwhelm the world.
MEPH I am a servant to great Lucifer,
　　　 And may not follow thee without his leave:
　　　 No more than he commands must we perform.
FAUST Did not he charge thee to appear to me?
MEPH No, I came now hither of mine own accord.
FAUST Did not my conjuring speeches raise thee? Speak.
MEPH That was the cause, but yet *per accidens*;
　　　 For, when we hear one rack the name of God,
　　　 Abjure the Scriptures and his Saviour Christ,
　　　 We fly, in hope to get his glorious soul;

Nor will we come, unless he use such means
Whereby he is in danger to be damn'd.
Therefore the shortest cut for conjuring
Is stoutly to abjure the Trinity,
And pray devoutly to the prince of hell.

FAUST So Faustus hath
Already done; and holds this principle,
There is no chief but only Belzebub;
To whom Faustus doth dedicate himself.
This word 'damnation' terrifies not him.
For he confounds hell in Elysium:
His ghost be with the old philosophers!
But, leaving these vain trifles of men's souls,
Tell me what is that Lucifer thy lord?

MEPH Arch-regent and commander of all spirits.

FAUST Was not that Lucifer an angel once?

MEPH Yes, Faustus, and most dearly lov'd of God.

FAUST How comes it, then, that he is prince of devils?

MEPH O, by aspiring pride and insolence;
For which God threw him from the face of heaven.

FAUST And what are you that live with Lucifer?

MEPH Unhappy spirits that fell with Lucifer,
Conspir'd against our God with Lucifer,
And are forever damn'd with Lucifer.

FAUST Where are you damn'd?

MEPH In hell.

FAUST How comes it, then, that thou are out of hell?

MEPH Why, this is hell, nor am I out of it.
Think'st thou that I, who saw the face of God,
And tasted the eternal joys of heaven,
Am not tormented with ten thousand hells,
In being depriv'd of everlasting bliss?
O, Faustus, leave these frivolous demands,
Which strike a terror to my fainting soul!

FAUST What, is great Mephistophilis so passionate
For being deprived of the joys of heaven?
Learn thou of Faustus manly fortitude,
And scorn those joys thou never shalt possess.
Go bear these tidings to great Lucifer:
Seeing Faustus hath incurr'd eternal death
By desperate thoughts against Jove's deity,
Say, he surrenders up to him his soul,
So he will spare him four-and-twenty years,
Letting him live in all voluptuousness;
Having thee ever to attend on me,
To give me whatsoever I shall ask,
To tell me whatsoever I demand,
To slay mine enemies, and aid my friends,
And always be obedient to my will.
Go and return to mighty Lucifer,
And meet me in my study at midnight,
And then resolve me of thy master's mind.

Many plays from the late sixteenth and early seventeenth centuries were the result of collaboration between two or more writers and the authorship of some surviving plays is not known. However, there is exciting material to be discovered in relatively obscure plays and we are including two speeches from the play *Lust's Dominion*, recently reintroduced at Shakespeare's Globe Theatre in London. The play is thought to be by Marlowe and, because it may be difficult for you to obtain a copy, we have included some of the plot summary:

Extract from *Lust's Dominion*

ELEAZAR is ruthless, resourceful and cunning, a brilliant Machiavellian figure, fit to place alongside Marlowe's BARABAS or Shakespeare's IAGO. Not only does he intend to destroy the Spanish royal family and all his enemies, but he has the vaunting ambition to wish to rule Spain himself. In his first soliloquy in Act 1 Scene 2, he makes all this clear to us:

ELEAZAR Old Time, I'll wait bareheaded at thy heels,
　　　And be a footboy to thy winged hours;
　　　They shall not tell one minute out in sands,
　　　But I'll set down the number ...
　　　Sweet opportunity! I'll bind myself
　　　To thee in base apprenticehood so long,
　　　Till on thy naked scalp grow hair as thick
　　　As mine; and all hands shall lay hold on thee,
　　　If thou wilt lend me but thy rusty scythe,
　　　To cut down all that stand within my wrongs
　　　And my revenge. Love, dance in twenty forms
　　　Upon my beauty, that this Spanish dame
　　　May be bewitch'd and dote; her amorous flames
　　　Shall blow up the old king, consume his sons,
　　　And make all Spain a bonfire.

Further Extract from *Lust's Dominion*

ELEAZAR's first and most durable victim is QUEEN EUGENIA, the Spanish dame to whom he refers. She is besotted with the young, virile MOOR and can be manipulated to carry out any crimes. We see this in the very first scene, where he appears to be tired of her. She should be with her dying husband, but has chosen to use a secret underground passage to be with the MOOR. She uses every device to coax him to kiss her:

QUEEN EUGENIA For each contracted frown
　　　A crooked wrinkle interlines my brow:
　　　Spend but one hour in frown, and I shall look
　　　Like to a beldame of one hundred years.
　　　I prythee, speak to me, and chide me not.
　　　I prythee, chide, if I have done amiss;
　　　But let my punishment be this and this.　　　　[*Kiss*
　　　Smile on me, and these two wanton boys,
　　　These pretty lads that do attend to me,

Shall call thee Jove, shall wait upon my cup,
And fill thee nectar: their enticing eyes
Shall serve as crystal, wherein thou may'st see
To dress thyself, if thou wilt smile on me.
Smile on me, and with coronets of pearl
And bells of gold, circling their pretty arms,
In a round ivory fount these two shall swim,
And dive to make thee sport:
Bestow one smile, one little, little smile,
And in a net of twisted silk and gold
In my all-naked arms thyself shall lie.

For further suggestions see after next section.

The Seventeenth Century:

In keeping with the international flavour of this collection, we have selected translations of speeches from the best-known dramatists of Spain (Calderon) and of France (Moliere).

In Calderon's play *The Great Stage of the World*, God is portrayed as a theatre director who gives human beings no script, but insists that they improvise! In many respects, this play shares characteristics with *Everyman* (see Medieval Theatre) with its allegorical figures and universal themes.

Extract from The Great Stage of the World

(From the translation by George Brandt.)

The DIRECTOR addresses WORLD.

DIRECTOR I being your Maker, you the thing I made,
　　　　I now wish to employ
　　　　You in a thing invented for my joy.
　　　　I mean to celebrate
　　　　My power infinitely great;
　　　　For does not mighty Nature find her sole delight
　　　　In showing forth my might?
　　　　Now as we know

That the most pleasing entertainment is a show,
And since we can
Interpret thus the entire Life of Man
I choose that Heaven shall today
Upon your stage witness a play.
I, being audience and manager together,
Can make the company perform this, whether
They would or not. And since
I have appointed Man the prince
Of all creation, for my company,
Mankind itself shall be
The actors that must show their arts
Upon *the stage of the world* which has four parts.
Each player I shall cast as I deem best,
And to ensure the play is to advantage dressed
With splendid costumes and with every machine
That may adorn the scene,
I wish you presently
To equip the stage with such machinery
As shall with fair effects take every eye,
Causing all doubt to fly
And giving the spectators certainty
Of faith in all they see.
And now it's time that we began –

I the Director, you the stage, the actor Man.

BEAUTY *addresses the* WORLD, HUMANITY *and the* AUDIENCE

BEAUTY Why do you want all things
     To be severe and cold?
     Is there no time for joy?
     Why else do you suppose
     Flowers were made by God
     If savouring their odour

Were barred to our smell?
Why did He make birds soar
Upon melodious wings
And cast enchantment forth
If hearing must not hear?
Why are there silken clothes
Delightful to the touch
If touch shall have no scope?
Why did He make rich fruits
Of sweetness all composed
If taste were not allowed?
Why did He furthermore
Make sun and sky and hills
And dales, if to behold
These sights were counted sin?
No, stubbornly to close
Our senses to His work
Marks an ungrateful soul.

Moliere's plays, with their witty criticism of contemporary society and its double standards, had a considerable influence on subsequent writing in English. You can capture their essence in performance if you can find a good translation in rhyming verse like the following version of *School for Wives* by Donald Frame:

Extract from *School for Wives* by Donald Frame

AGNESS, a young and 'innocent' woman, makes one of many outrageous speeches to ARNOLPHE, her guardian.

AGNESS It's quite amazing, quite hard to believe.
    Out on the balcony to get the air,
    I saw, under those trees right over there,
    A most attractive young man passing by,
    Who bowed most humbly when he caught my eye.

And I, not wishing to be impolite,
Returned a deep bow, as was only right.
Promptly he makes another bow, and then,
I naturally bow to him again;
And since he then goes on to number three,
Without delay he gets a third from me.
He passes by, comes back ... well, anyhow,
Each time he does he makes another bow.
And I, observing this most carefully,
Returned him every bow he made to me.
The fact is, if the light had not grown dim,
I would have gone on trading bows with him,
Because I did not want to yield, and be
Inferior to him in courtesy.

Further Suggestions:

Speeches by ALICE in *Arden of Faversham* by 'Mr. S.', by Susan and Cuddy in *The Witch of Edmonton* by Rowley and Middleton.

Many roles in drama of this period are for men, but for girls there are splendid speeches for PUCK (Act II Sc 2) and HELENA (same) in *A Midsummer Night's Dream*, VIOLA (Act II Sc 2) in *Twelfth Night*, PHEBE (Act III Sc 5) in *As You Like It* and for JULIET throughout *Romeo and Juliet*.

Look also at ISABELLA (Act IV Sc 2) in Kyd's *The Spanish Tragedy*, LEVIDULCIA (Act IV Sc 5) in Tourneur's *The Atheist's Tragedy* and ZENOCRATE (Part 1. Act V Sc 2) in Marlowe's *Tamburlaine the Great*.

For Scenes for two girls there is wonderful material in:

- PUCK and the FAIRY (Act II Sc I) in *A Midsummer Night's Dream*.
- VIOLA and OLIVIA (Act I Sc 5 line 169 onwards) in *Twelfth Night*.
- CELIA and ROSALIND (e.g. Act III Sc 2) and throughout *As You Like It*.
- MISTRESS PAGE and MISTRESS FORD throughout *The Merry Wives of Windsor*.
- JUNO and VENUS (Act III Sc 2) in Marlowe's *Dido Queen of Carthage*.
- JULIET and the NURSE (Act II Sc 5) in *Romeo and Juliet*.
- EMILIA and DESDEMONA (Act I V Sc 3) in *Othello*.

The Eighteenth Century:

Following the example of the French theatre, many of the English plays of this period were concerned with marriage and domestic issues. The appearance of actresses on the London stage for the first time in the late seventeenth century ensured that subsequent plays had substantial roles for women. Many of the stage conventions from this time, including 'cross dressing' and 'asides', have been preserved in the pantomimes that are now popular at Christmas.

Congreve's *The Way of the World* introduces the lively character of Mrs Marwood – here is one of several suitable speeches:

Extract from *The Way of the World*

Enter MRS MARWOOD

MRS MARWOOD   Indeed, Mrs Engine, is it thus with you? are you become a go-between of this importance? yes, I shall watch you. Why this wench is the *passé-partout*, a very master key to everybody's strongbox. My friend Fainall, have you carried it so swimmingly? I thought there was something in it; but it seems 'tis over with you. Your loathing is not from a want of appetite then, but from a surfeit. Else you could never be so cool to fall from a principal to be an assistant; to procure for him! a pattern of generosity, that, I confess. Well, Mr Fainall, you have met with your match. – O man, man! woman, woman! the devil's an ass: if I were a painter, I would draw him like an idiot, a driveller with a bib and bells. Man should have his head and horns, and woman the rest of him. Poor simple fiend! – 'Madam Marwood has a month's mind, but he can't abide her.' – 'Twere better for him you had not been his confessor in that affair, without you could have kept his counsel closer. I shall not prove another pattern of generosity; he has not obliged me to that with those excesses of himself! and now I'll have none of him. Here comes the good Lady, panting ripe; with a heart full of hope, and a head full of care, like any chemist upon the day of projection.

The prologue for *The School for Scandal* by the Irish dramatist R. B. Sheridan could be spoken by a performer of either sex and the play itself contains many effective speeches for individuals.

N.B. This speech was written by the leading actor to introduce Sheridan's play:

Extract from *The Scool for Scandal*

Prologue by Mr Garrick

SIR PETER TEAZLE A School for Scandal! tell me, I beseech you,
 Needs there a school this modish art to teach you?
 No need of lesson now, the knowing think;
 We might as well be taught to eat and drink.
 Caused by a dearth of scandal, should the vapors
 Distress our fair ones – let them read the papers;
 Their powerful mixtures such disorders hit;
 Crave what you will – there's quantum sufficit[1.]
 'Lord!' cries my Lady Wormwood (who loves tattle,
 And puts much salt and pepper in her prattle).
 Just risen at noon, all night at cards when threshing
 Strong tea and scandal – 'Bless me, how refreshing!
 Give me the papers, Lisp – how bold and free!   [*Sips*
 Last night Lord L. – [*sips*] was caught with Lady D.
 For aching heads what charming *sal volatile!*   [*Sips*
 If Mrs B. will still continue flirting,
 We hope she'll DRAW, *or we'll* UNDRAW *the curtain.*
 Fine satire, po z[2] – in public all abuse it,
 But, by ourselves – [*sips*], our praise we can't refuse it.
 Now, Lisp, read you – there are that dash and star.'
 'Yes, ma'am – A certain Lord had best beware,
 Who lives not twenty miles for Grosvenor Square;
 For should he Lady W. find willing,
 Wormwood is bitter' – 'Oh! that's me! the villain!
 Throw it behind the fire, and never more
 Let that vile paper come within my door.'

Thus at our friends we laugh, who feel the dart;
To reach our feelings, we ourselves must smart.
Is our young bard so young, to think that he
Can stop the full springtide of calumny!
Knows he the world so little, and its trade?
Alas! the devil's sooner and raised that laid.
So strong, so swift, the monster there's no gagging:
Cut Scandal's head off, still the tongue is wagging.
Proud of your smiles once lavishly bestowed,
Again our young Don Quixote takes the road;
To show his gratitude he draws his pen,
And seeks his hydra, Scandal, in his den.
For your applause all perils he would through –
He'll fight – that's write – a cavalliero true,
Till every drop of blood – that's ink – is spilt for you.

Notes:
1 Plenty
2 Positively

The Nineteenth Century:

Drama of the nineteenth-century covers a vast range of styles: from the sentimental melodramas, popular throughout Europe and the English-speaking world: through the early attempts to write serious, realistic drama, to the intense psychological realism of the plays of the Swedish playwright Strindberg and the Norwegian dramatist Ibsen. Both these playwrights had a profound effect on subsequent writers and it is from their time that we usually date 'modern drama'.

T. W. Robertson was nicknamed 'doorknobs Robertson', because of his obsession with realistic details in stage settings. His play, *Caste*, is a good example of a play seeking to address a serious social issue: in this case, class structure.

I am including the stage directions in the next extract simply to help you understand the context of the piece:

Extract from *Caste*

POLLY ECCLES enjoys little social standing as an actress and the play gives a particularly vivid picture of life in the nineteenth-century theatre.

SCENE. *The room in Stangate (as in Act I). Same furniture as in Act I with exception of piano, with roll of music tied up on it in place of bureau, R. Map of India over mantelpiece. Sword with crape knot, spurs, and cap, craped, hanging over chimney-piece. Portrait of* D'ALROY *(large) on mantelpiece Berceaunette, and child, with coral, in it.* POLLY'S *bonnet and shawl hanging on peg, R. flat. Small tin saucepan in fender, fire alight, and kettle on it. Two candles (tallow) in sticks, one of which is broken about three inches from the top and hangs over. Slate and pencil on table. Jug on table, bandbox and ballet skirt on table.*

At rise of curtain POLLY discovered at table, back of stage, Comes down and places skirt in bandbox. She is dressed in black.

POLLY [*placing skirt in box and leaning her child upon her hand*] There – there's the dress for poor Esther in case she gets the engagement, which I don't suppose she will. It's too good luck, and good luck never comes to her, poor thing. [*Goes up to back of cradle*] Baby's asleep still. How good he looks – as good as if he were dead, like his poor father; and alive too, at the same time, like his dear self. Ah! dear me; it's a strange world. [*Sits in chair R. of table, feeling in pocket for money*] Four and eleven pence. That must do for today and tomorrow. Esther is going to bring in the rusks for Georgy. [*Takes up slate*] Three, five–eight, and four– twelve, one shilling – father can only have two pence [*this all to be said in one breath*], he must make do with that till Saturday, when I get my salary. If Esther gets the engagement, I shan't have many more salaries to take; I shall leave the stage and retire into private life. I wonder if I shall like private life, and if private life will like me. It will seem so strange being no longer Miss Mary Eccles – but Mrs Samuel Gerridge. [*Writes it on slate*] 'Mrs Samuel Gerridge.' [*Laughs bashfully*] La! to think of my being Mrs

Anybody. How annoyed Susan Smith will be! [*Writing on slate*] 'Mrs Samuel Gerridge presents her compliments to Miss Susan Smith, and Mrs Samuel Gerridge requests the favour of Miss Susan Smith's company to tea, on Tuesday evening next, at Mrs Samuel Gerridge's house.' [*Pause*] Poor Susan! [*Beginning again*] 'P.S. – Mrs Samuel Gerridge –'

[*Knock heard at room door;* POLLY *starts*

Strindberg's play *Miss Julie* also confronts the problem of class. The aristocratic Miss Julie has an affair with her servant Jean. These two extracts in the translation by Arvid Paulson, demonstrate the passionate tensions that exist between the two characters. There are many good, recent versions that you should also explore:

Extract from *Miss Julie*

MISS JULIE You don't mean what you say – and besides: everybody knows my secrets. You see, my mother was not an aristocrat by birth. She came of quite simple stock. She was brought up in conformity with the ideas of her generation: equality of the sexes – the emancipation of women – and all that sort of thing. She looked upon marriage with downright aversion. Therefore, when my father proposed marriage to her, she replied that she would never be his wife – but she married him just the same. I came into the world – against my mother's wishes, as I have learned; and now I was to be reared by my mother as a child of nature and in addition was to be taught all the things a boy has to learn, all in order to prove that a woman is quite as good as any man. I had to wear boy's clothes, had to learn how to handle horses, but I was never allowed in the cattle barn. I had to groom, harness and saddle my horse and had to go hunting – yes, I even had to try my hand at farming! And the farmhands were given women's chores to do, and the women did the men's work – and the upshot of it was that the estate almost went to rack and ruin, and we became the laughing-stock of the whole countryside ... At last my father seems to have come out of his inertia, for he rebelled; and after that all went according to his will. My mother took sick – what the sickness was I never learned – but she frequently had spasms, shut herself up in the attic, or secluded herself in the garden – and sometimes she stayed out all night. Then came the great fire which you have heard about. The house, the stables, and the cattle barns burned down, and under suspicious circumstances that pointed to arson. The disaster happened, namely, the day after the quarterly insurance period had expired; and the insurance premium, that my father had forwarded by a messenger, had arrived too late because of the messenger's negligence or indifference.

[She fills up her glass and drinks

JEAN You mustn't drink any more!

MISS JULIE Ah, what do I care! – We were left with nothing, and we had no place to sleep, except in the carriages.

MISS JULIE [*seats herself*] How priceless!

JEAN Yes, you may call it that! It was preposterous! – You see – it was that incident I was loath to tell you about, a moment ago – but now I shall ... Do you know how your world looks from below? No, you don't. Like hawks and falcons – whose backs we rarely see because they are always soaring high up in the sky ... I lived in my father's little shack with seven brothers and sisters and one pig out in the grey, barren fields where not even a tree grew. But from the windows I could see the wall enclosing the count's park, with the apple trees rising about it. That was to me the Garden of Eden; and it was protected by a multitude of fierce angels with flaming swords. In spite of their presence, I and some other boys found our way to the tree of life ... Now you despise me, don't you?

MISS JULIE Heavens, no – all boys steal apples!

JEAN You say so now, but you have contempt for me just the same ... Well – one time I went into the Garden of Paradise with my mother, to weed the onion beds. Near the vegetable garden there was a Turkish pavilion standing in the shade of jasmine, and overgrown with honeysuckle. I had no idea what it could be used for; but I had never seen such a beautiful building ... People went inside, then came out again; and one day the door was left open. I sneaked in and saw the walls were covered with pictures of emperors and kings; and, hanging at the windows were red curtains with tassels. Now you understand where I was ... I ... [*he breaks off a spray of lilac and holds it close to her nostrils*] I had never been inside the castle, and had never seen any place as grand as the church, but this was if anything more beautiful ... And no matter which way my thoughts went, they always returned to – to that place ... And gradually it developed into a yearning to experience some day all of its splendour and charm. – *Enfin*, I stole inside, gazed and admired, but just then I heard someone coming! There was only one exit for cultivated people – but for me there was another; and I had no choice but to take it ...

> [*MISS JULIE, who meanwhile has accepted the lilac spray from JEAN, lets it drop on the tape*

JEAN ... and then I took to my heels, plunged through a raspberry hedge, dashed across the strawberry patches and found myself on the rose terrace. There I gazed at a figure in pink dress and white stockings – it was you. I hid underneath a heap of weeds and lay there – lay there, imagine, with thistles pricking me and under dank, stinking earth. If it is true that a thief can get to heaven and be with the angels, why should it be impossible for a poor peasant child here on God's earth, to get into the castle park and play with the count's daughter ...

Further Suggestions:

Candida or *Saint Joan* by G. B. Shaw, *The Colleen Bawn* by Dion Boucicault. Any plays in *Nineteeth Century Plays* Ed. George Rowell (London, OUP).

The Twentieth and Twenty-first Centuries:

The twentieth century produced a huge body of dramatic writing in almost every country and continent in which English is spoken, together with a renewed interest in, and a rediscovery of ancient forms of, drama from all over the world. You should investigate the writing from your own country as a priority, but the following constitutes a small collection of suitable lesser-known material.

Anthea Preston's play *Vita and Harold* explores the remarkable marriage between the British diplomat Harold Nicholson and the poet Vita Sackville-West, using their letters and diaries as the basis of the text. Here is part of the opening of the play that involves a 'flashback' to former years:

Extract from *Vita and Harold*

[*30th September, 1946*
Grand Hotel, Paris

HAROLD Tomorrow we shall have been married 33 years. I shall send you a telegram. If I put 'loving thoughts', the French telegraphists will get it wrong; but if I put '*tendres amities*', they will get muddled at Cranbrook. So I shall put it in Aramaic. Oh my dearest Viti, what a long life we have had together and what a happy, busy, profitable, useful one! I know that our love for each other is as enduring as life. We may die, we may go off our heads, we may take to drugs, we may be put in prison, we may grow the most dreadful carbuncles – but we shall love each other absolutely until d.d.u.p.

VITA My darling fellow-traveller; how oddly life turns out … There were you and me, sitting on Angela Manners' hat box in the attics of Hatfield. And now we are going off to Djakarta, 40-odd years later, loving each other far more deeply and wisely than we did then, and with our sons- and daughters-in-law, and granddaughters growing up and making their own lives for themselves.

That is all very pleasing; but what pleases me more than anything is that you and I, after all the mistakes and infidelities and errors we have both made in our lives, should now be closer than ever we were ...

It is rather nice to embark on a honeymoon again, after 47 years. Yes?   [*Exchange look*

                                        [*Putting on hat and coming centre front*

VITA   IT all began that night at the Hatfield Ball – he asked me to marry him and I said I would. He was very shy, and pulled all the buttons one by one off his gloves; I was frightened and tried to prevent him from coming to the point.

He didn't kiss me, but we sat, rather bewildered, over supper afterwards and talked excitedly, though vaguely, about the flat we would have in Rome. I had on a new dress.

Harold was a delightful companion

                                        [*Reading from notebook*

    And in the dews beside me
    Behold a youth that trod
    With feathered cap on forehead,
    And poised a golden rod,
    With mien to match the morning,
    And gay delightful guise ...

                              [*HAROLD joins VITA, offering her his arm.*
                              Stand together as if in church

HAROLD We were married at Knole on the 1st October 1913 and to everybody's intense delight Vita's mother B.M., as she was always called, stayed in bed all day. In the chapel our eyes met and it flashed into our minds that this was the most tremendous lark out of which we must get the most fun possible.

                                        [*HAROLD returns to room*

VITA My only qualms before the wedding were about leaving my beloved Knole –   [Quoting

152

I left you in the crowds and in the light
And if I laughed or sorrowed none could tell
They could not know our true and deep farewell
Was spoken in the long preceding night ...

[*VITA freezes*

The 'Lewis and Clark' Expedition is remembered as one of the great pioneering events in the history of the United States. Captains Meriwether Lewis and William Clark left Fort Manda (in present day North Dakota) in the spring of 1805 and arrived at the mouth of the Columbia River in November of that year. Captain Clark's slave York was a significant member of the expedition and the contemporary American playwright Bryan Harnetiaux and the actor and drummer David Casteal have told his story in their play *York*.

Here is the opening speech:

Extract from *York*

At rise: A make-shift tavern/livery stable in St Louis, circa 1811, where Abolitionists and Freedmen gather. There is a hand-painted sign that says 'YORK TONITE'. A drummed heartbeat in the darkness slowly builds in tempo. Lights up on YORK, eyes closed, drumming. As the heartbeat nears a fevered pitch, his eyes snap open.

YORK My heart tole me somethin' was wrong. Poundin' so hard, woke me up. Near five years ago – summer a '05. Only there's a foot a snow an' flakes comin' down big's flapjacks. And we're all buried in it 'round the camp pit, with a fire tha's dead out. Except Pryor, who's sittin' 'neath a tree on guard duty, rifle 'cross his lap – froze up. I'm thinkin' the Captain 'ill give him the lash for sure, if he ain't dead already. I climb outa my bag. It's a mean snow. Summer snow, Rocky Mountain kind. I go on over to Pryor, kinda protected under this tree. His face's all glazed over. I shake him, an' it sounds like fine china breakin' into pieces. Take my knife and go to chipping the ice away around his eyes an' mouth, 'til I hear this small sound inside him. Like it's coming from down aroun' his knees. He's in there, barely. I straighten him up an' lean him 'gainst a tree, dig around and find the axe an' flint. Cut underbrush 'neath every limb I can find. Then I clear out the pit an' flint it up and pretty soon it's roarin' good. Then I hurry an' cut a coupla strong yokes and drive 'em in on each side a the fire pit, find a limb and tie Pryor to it and lift him up on the yokes over the fire. So I can turn him some, thaw him out. 'Tween turns I dig up Captain Clark and Cap Lewis an' the others, an' stack 'em up next to the pit. I'm dusting the Captain off 'cause I figure he'll be next, bein' I'm responsible for him, when Pryor starts a hollerin' like a banshee. So I know he's done. I'm liftin' him off to get the Captain situated on the spit when there's a hellish roar and this she bear comes a bustin' outa the trees, headin' straight for Captain Clark. Now, this ain' no regular bear. Make a Kentuck black bear look like a house cat. Well, she sees me an' pulls up sudden like, not three feet away. Standin' on her haunches, eight to ten feet high, teeth long as icicles. An' as she's a ponderin' this black creature, one hand brings my knife up through her middle an' the other reaches in an' yanks her heart out an' shows it to her – still beatin'. That old sow she just nods – almost smiles – an' drops like an oak. Shakes the ground so hard the Captain falls off the spit an' thrashes around in the fire, 'fore I drag him out.

YORK spots an unseen CAPTAIN CLARK as he enters the tavern/livery

YORK [*sees CLARK*] Speak a the devil.

[*Returning to his story*

His hair's a bit singed, but he's fine. I 'member Captain laying there, steam comin' off, staring up at me – lookin' one part mad, the other right grateful-like.

[*YORK acknowledges the unseen Clark again*

You 'member that Captain? Gentlemen, Captain William Clark, a the Lewis an' Clark Expedition. Yessuh. Now that ain't the look I'm talkin' about.

> [*Mimicking* CLARK's *arms-folded military stance*

Tha' your 'bes' come with me or else' look. Don' believe I will, Captain. Maybe you'd like ta tell these fellas one a your own stories 'bout the expedition an' all. Fine by me.

> [*YORK exits the tavern/livery stable for another time and place, glancing back at* CLARK *as he leaves*

The play *Promenade* by the Cuban-born dramatist Maria Irene Fornes was first performed in the fringe theatres of New York, often labelled the 'Underground Theater'. This highly experimental, short play is partly written in verse and is set in a prison. The prisoners have no names, only numbers, and the other characters are simply known as MISS I, etcetera.

In this scene, the prisoners are in the park:

Extract from *Promenade*

MISS I [*opening her arms toward 105 and 106*] Let's you and me embrace.

> [*105 and 106 are confused as to which one she means. They bump against each other, bow to each other, offer the way to the other. They finally get to her with open arms*

The moment has passed.
You have, perhaps, made me feel something
But the moment has passed.
And what is done cannot be undone.
Once a moment passes, it never comes again.

I once had a man who loved me well.
His mouth was smaller than his eye.
But I loved him just the same.
Yes, I loved him just the same.

He said he would kill for me.
And I said like for instance whom?
And he said like for instance you
Like for instance you.

Sometimes it hurts more than others.
Sometimes it hurts less.
Sometimes it's just the same.
Sometimes it's really just the same.
But never mind that.
No never mind that.
God gave understanding just to confuse us.
And it's always the same, anyway.
It's always the same, anyway.

If it's in your path to hurt me,
By all means do.
But, I beg you don't go out of your way.
Don't go out of your way to do so.

You don't know what to make of me.
But I know what to make of you.
I've nothing to lose
Or not much, anyway.
But never mind that,
God gave understanding just to confuse us.
And it's always the same, anyway.

You have, perhaps, made me feel something
But the moment has passed.
And what is done cannot be undone.
Once a moment passes, it never comes again.   [*She exits*

Jennifer Johnston is one of several talented contemporary playwrights from Northern Ireland. This is a monologue from her play *The Desert Lullaby*.

Extract from *The Desert Lullaby*

FLORA I am a woman alone.
   That was what mother used to say to make us feel bad.
   Your father is battling in the desert and I am a woman alone.
   You have to help me by being very, very good.
   She used to say it to visitors also.
   Paul is battling in the desert. Then she would give a little laugh.
   Paul, Father, Daddy.
   It was such a brave little laugh; and then someone would take
   her hand or touch her lightly on the shoulder, or just give a little
   sigh. It was his second war.
   I used to feel quite sorry for him, when I thought of that.
   He got the tail end of the first one. Eighteen, straight from
   school.
   There are pictures of him all round the house, looking so
   handsome in his uniform.
   So ...
   He was my dear friend.
   He never explained to me though why he felt he had to go and
   leave us all. Leave poor mother to be a woman alone.
   I missed him so much when he went away.
   I missed him so much when he never came back.
   He had this wonderful, hearty laugh. He used to throw his head
   right back and roar with laughter. Eddie used to do that, too. He
   had that same laugh.
   At night, I used to lie in bed and listen and, from time to time,
   that laugh of his would come running to me all the way up
   the stairs.
   he would lift me in his arms and put his lips to the side of my
   neck and blow warm air into my skin. I remember shivering with
   joy when he did that.

You'll ruin that child, Paul, mother would say.

I dreamed that I would marry him when I grew up; all in white like she had been. White lace dipping to the ground at the back and shorter in the front, showing elegant white satin shoes.

Chicken, I will love you forever, he said in my dreams and blew warm air on my neck.

Bye, chicken was what he'd said when he left, we'll meet again some sunny day. Then he threw back his head and laughed. He never even mentioned the possibility of death.

I was not in any way prepared for that.

El Alamein.

We had this map of North Africa on a table in the drawing room, with all those names on it: Tobruk, Mersa Matruh, Hemiemat, Benghazi, El Alamein.

After we got the news, she drew a little black cross by El Alamein in indelible pencil, because she wasn't able at that moment to find her pen. A few days later, she rolled up the map and put it away as if the war didn't exist any more.

We don't need any more of that was what she said.

We learnt about Khartoum at school; about General Gordon and all that sort of thing. I put up my hand and asked if Khartoum was anywhere near El Alamein.

No, said Miss Ross, Africa is rather a large place you know, Flora, and everyone giggled.

I would like to have told them about him, about the black cross in indelible pencil, but the words stuck in my mouth. Dry words, like biscuit crumbs, stuck to the roof of my mouth.

Maybe it's just as well. Sometimes there are things you should just keep to yourself.

I have already introduced you to the *Epic of Gilgamesh* earlier in the book (see p89) and it can be presented as prose or as your own dramatised version. The next extract is from a stage adaptation by the Caravan of Dreams Theater, who also made the adaptation of *Marouf the Cobbler* used earlier in this collection:

Extract from *Epic of Gilgamesh*

SCENE 6

NIMSUN accompanied by two temple dancers; GILGAMESH, ENKIDU enter

GILGAMESH Mother, the counsellors of the city moan at Enkidu and me.
    They say you are young, foolhardy, you don't understand what
    going to seek out Humbaba means.
NIMSUN You are going to attack Humbaba?
GILGAMESH They say
    Humbaba does not die like men
    His weapons are invincible
    His roar is like flood
    His breath like the forest fire
    His jaws are death.
    Why do you wish to do this, Gilgamesh?
    Humbaba does not fight fairly.
ENKIDU Gilgamesh answered,
    He laughed at the counsellors
    He asked me,
    Shall I answer that I am afraid of Humbaba
    That I shall be a stay-at-home
    Fat and afraid as these men?
GILGAMESH I said we shall go to Nimsun
    Nimsun the Queen knows the deep knowledge,
    She must give us counsel.
    Now, Nimsun, listen to me;
    I must travel a long journey,
    To the Forest of Humbaba,

To fight no common fight.

NIMSUN [*putting on her finest costume, lighting incense*] O Sun,
Why did you give this restless heart
To Gilgamesh, my son, why?
Now he sets out on a long journey,
To the Forest of Humbaba,
On an unknown road
To fight no common fight.
So from the moment he leaves,
Until he reaches the Forest of Cedars,
Until he kills Humbaba,
O Sun, do not forget him;
Let the dawn remind you daily,
Give him sleep each night.

[*She puts out incense*

Enkidu,
You are not my body's child,
But you shall be like my child,

[*Places amulet around his neck*

I trust my son with you.
Bring him back safely.

[*They leave*

Advanced Prose:

In this selection of prose passages I have included material of three main types: prose in which the thoughts and feelings of the writer predominate (sometimes called 'lyric' or 'lyrical' prose); prose with a strong narrative intention and prose which presents an argument or makes some attempt to influence opinion.

Wherever performance takes place in our modern world there remains concern over the effects of climate change and of the impact of technology in a rapidly changing environment. In the following passage from the second volume of *Wind in the Pylons*, the author takes the basis of a children's story and makes it into a powerful parable for our age. You could argue that this passage embraces all three of the types of prose I have mentioned above and this indicates that such divisions are never concrete.

Extract from *The Wind in the Pylons*

The Mole was wakened unreasonably early the next morning by an unseasonably early cuckoo. But against all the odds he had slept well in the night, pleased to be so independent and capable of coping, too. (He had heated up some powdery dry-stuff with water on the stove and it had warmed him: through the disturbing strangeness, it had tasted almost like food.)

So it was with some vigour that he unzipped and flipped his rip-stop zip-flap and stumbled out from his tent with a sense of freshness and latent energy that might perhaps be harnessed (though not, of course, until well after breakfast): a sense of new horizons that could ... that could perhaps be crossed.

'You're before your season!' he told that cuckoo. 'Aren't you? You're at least a fortnight early!'

'Phupp-poo!' responded the cuckoo, one hundred per cent invisible in the depths of a shrubbery, as cuckoos always are.

The Mole decided he should begin his first morning as he meant to go on, and try to make some use over breakfast of the magical voice-box which Justin had lent to him: it did seem to be a valuable source of information about the world. The Mole persisted in calling this device a "voice-box" despite the fact that Justin had told him, four or five times, that it was a "ray-jo". In his heart of hearts, the Mole felt the word "ray-jo" was just a little silly: his own word was not only more dignified, it was also a rather better description of what the thing was.

But how to work it? That was the problem. He stared at the small black object and its arcane layout of buttons and numbers. 'Just move the POWER switch to ON!' Justin had explained to him despairingly. '"POWER"? – See? ... "ON" ... there? That's it – yes! N ... N ... Yessss ...!' Nervously the Mole slid the little black thing to the right with the tip of a claw and nearly dropped the box as a voice jumped out of it, so loud it seemed the object might vibrate itself apart. He jammed it off again. 'Too loud! ... MUCH too loud!' said the Mole. Then, recalling other instructions, he fumbled apprehensively with another little black-thing marked as "VOLUME" and tried again.

'... reports coming in,' said a by now not unfamiliar, ebullient voice – very clear, not too loud, not too soft – 'of what is feared may be a major chemicals spill from the huge Toad Transoceanic complex in northern Teesside. Our north-east correspondent Mike Moledredge is already at the scene – at the other end of a Deracitel, unfortunately ... Mike, can you hear me?'

'Yes, John,' shouted another much less distinct voice, fading in and fading out through crackles, '... there has been a leakage here ... we know it is from an acid storage unit at the edge of the complex, though we don't have any other details yet ... ver several miles of coastal marshland ... ly this appears to be a very serious incident, and local naturalists fear ... ny years, if ever, before ... could return to a healthy state ... huge area of marine life could be threat ...'

'– Mike ... sorry to interrupt you there. You're breaking up on us, I'm afraid. We'll try to get back to you later on. NOW – the time is: six forty-seven precisely. And appropriately enough, perhaps, after that last report, we have here now one of the rising young stars of the influential Mart-wing think tank the Feral Studies Institute, Mr Farris Ferris, who is to give a talk later on today at the London Temple of Economics in which he will be putting forward the challenging idea that even the future existence of plant and animal species could eventually be decided through the actions of the Market – Can this be right, Mr Ferris?'

'I believe that's now pretty clear,' drawled a much lighter, boyish voice. 'Yaahh. What we have to recognise, I think, is that it's in the power of the Market-Mystery to be able to determine every last detail of our impacts on the world we live in –'

'– But not, *surely*,' interrupted the first voice, 'whether there are still tigers in the jungle, say? Or butterflies flapping about in the fields? Some would argue, wouldn't they, that that kind of thing is a matter for Nature alone? Just so long as we don't mess it all up in the first place, of course?'

'The real issue, John – one I think we should start to grasp –' breathed Mr Ferris in tones of airiest detachment, 'is this: the world is becoming increasingly global. You mentioned fields. Every field is a workplace, isn't it? And your other example, the jungle? Every sector of jungle on the planet may and indeed can be regarded – with reference to vastatabulatagram produced for us by the BCF at Cambridge University –'

Many sacred and mystical writings from religious texts verge on poetry, but are a form of lyrical prose. It is recommended that you should explore the writings associated with your own faith, although we have included some material from a number of sources. The first extract is from *The Hermetica*: a collection of writings attributed to an ancient Egyptian sage Thoth, who was known in Egypt in 3000 BCE. These works were very influential in Renaissance Europe, but then disappeared, only to be rediscovered in 1945:

Extract from *Hermetica*

The Birth of Human Culture

Humanity looked in awe upon the beauty and everlasting duration of creation. The exquisite sky flooded with sunlight. The majesty of the dark night, lit by celestial torches as the holy planetary powers trace their paths in the heavens in fixed and steady metre – ordering the growth of things with their secret infusions. Men looked with wonder and questioning, and, having observed the Maker's masterpiece, wanted to create things for themselves. Their Father gave permission, so the gods who administer the Cosmos each shared with humanity a part of their power.

Since the world is Atum's handiwork, those who maintain and enhance its beauty are cooperating with the will of Atum by contributing their bodily strength in daily care and labour to make things assume the shape which his purpose has designed. Chance is movement without order, and skill is the force which creates order.

The Bible is still the best-selling book in the world today. The first part of the book: the *Old Testament,* deals with the Jewish faith from which Christianity largely developed. As we have already seen (see p. 95) there are many translations of the Bible and you should find your own preferred version. Some of the most intense, lyrical passages are found in the Psalms and you may find that Psalm 8 (particularly in the Authorised or 'King James' version) reminds you of words from Shakespeare's *Hamlet.* Here it is in a modern version:

Extract from *The Good News Bible*

God's Glory and Man's Dignity

O LORD, our Lord,
your greatness is seen in all the world!
Your praise reaches up to the heavens;
it is sung by children and babies.
You are safe and secure from all your enemies;
you stop anyone who opposes you.

When I look at the sky, which you have made,
at the moon and the stars, which you set in their places –
what is man, that you think of him;
mere man, that you care for him?

Yet you made him inferior only to yourself;
you crowned him with glory and honour.
You appointed him ruler over everything you made;
you placed him over all creation:
sheep and cattle, and the wild animals, too;
the birds and the fish
and the creatures in the seas.

The following traditional Muslim prayer is attributed to Ali, the cousin of Muhammad and the fourth Cailif of Islam. He is particularly venerated by Shi'ah Muslims:

Extract from (Prayer title?)

(Adapted from an Arabic text by Ken Pickering.)

O God, I am looking for refuge with Thee, in case I am like a servant who, knowing Thy mysteries, did not repent fully but returned to transgression. Make this penitence such that I do not need to repent again but may dwell securely with Thee

O God, I acknowledge my ignorance to you: I have nothing but my wrong-doing to bring to you. In Thy patience, take me into the shelter of Thy mercy and hide me graciously with the curtain of Thy forgiveness.

O my God, I regret all the thoughts, sights and words that contravene Thy love and Thy will.

Have mercy upon me, O God, in my lonely state. My heart is troubled and my frame is anguished when I think of Thee. If I were to keep silent there would be no-one to speak for me and I have no grounds to plead.

Spread Thy mercy around me like a veil and hide me in Thy glory. Do with me as a great one would who heard the pleas of a helpless, poor servant and refreshed him. Because, O God, I have no defender from your justice. Only Thy goodness can be my defence and intercessor. My wrong deeds have made me afraid, but, Thy pardon can give me peace.

Patrick Leigh Fermor's autobiographical book *A Time of Gifts* contains both lyrical and narrative passages: indeed, there is scarcely a page that does not ask to be read aloud. Expelled from his school in Canterbury, England, for having an affair with a greengrocer's daughter, the author set out to walk across Europe to Constantinople (modern Istanbul) in the years just before the Second World War. I include two extracts:

Extract from *A Time of Gifts*

The writer sometimes found hospitality with families or individuals who then sent on a note of introduction to friends or relatives along the way. When the note did not arrive an awkward situation was created!
In describing his journey, Patrick Fermor frequently employs lyrical prose.

It was the eleventh of February, the morning of my nineteenth birthday. As I still had festive notions about anniversaries, I had planned to spend the end of it under a friendly roof. Not that Paul's wasn't; but, before setting out from Dürrenstein, I had telephoned to some more friends of Baron Liphart who lived an easy half-day's walk from Göttweig. The line had been bad and the faint voice of the Gräfin at the other end sounded a bit surprised. But she managed to convey across the chaotic wires that they longed for news of their old friend in Munich. I was expected about teatime.

It snowed and blew all the way. The Schloss, when it took shape at last through the whirling flakes, really was a castle. It was a huge sixteenth-century pile with a moat and battlements surrounded by a wide white park. Its dark towers would have awed Childe Roland; they called for a blast of the slughorn. I battled my way there and found a man shovelling out a path that filled up again as fast as he dug, and asked him, at the top of my voice, where the front door was – it was snowing too hard to see much in the falling dark. Which Count did I want, he bawled back: what Christian name? It sounded as if there were two or more brothers about: mine was Graf Joseph; he led me into a courtyard. I was caked and clogged and thatched like a snowman, and when I got into the hall a grey-green butler helped me to beat and brush it off, hospitality seconded by Graf Joseph, who had come down the stairs.

This was all very well. But, from the friendly but puzzled faces of my hosts, I understood that, apart from my all-but-inaudible telephone conversation, they had no notion of any impending visit. No letter had reached them from Munich. My telephone call had conveyed an impression, I think, of some Englishman motoring to Vienna proposing himself for tea or a drink. Instead of this urbane imaginary absentee, they were confronted by an affable tramp with a knapsack and hobnailed boots. When we had been talking about our Munich friends for half an hour, a moment of silence prolonged itself for a few seconds; and, during the gap made by this angel's overflight, a swarm of anxieties and doubts and uncharacteristic scruples rushed into my mind. I felt suddenly convinced that they longed to be alone. Perhaps they had just heard bad news; other visitors might be expected at any moment; or they might simply be bored stiff: why not? Anyway, I was convinced that a stranger's presence might be a curse past bearing, and this loss of nerve gave way to a touch of insanity: *perhaps they thought I was a burglar?* I heard myself clumping to my feet and inventing, in a strangled voice, an excuse for departure. I had to catch a train that night, I said, in order to meet a friend arriving in Vienna by train next day. The unconvincing lameness and confusion of this invention called up looks of surprise, then bewilderment and finally concern as though they had a mild lunatic on their hands. At which station was I meeting my friend? Desperately, and at a venture, I said, the Western one ... luckily, a *Westbahnhof did* exist. When was I meeting this friend? 'Oh – at noon.' 'Then *that's* all right,' they said. 'You can't possibly go on tonight in weather like this! We'll get you to the station in plenty of time for your rendezvous in Vienna.' I think it must have been obvious that the entire rigmarole was nonsense, but none of us could say so. They may have guessed that it had been prompted by diffidence. My fears had been chimerical; but I was committed to my mythical programme. In spite of all this, dinner and the evening were easy and delightful. When I outlined my future journey, they were full of suggestions, my hostess made me take down the names and addresses of kinsmen and friends on the way who might help, especially in Hungary, and she promised to write to them.

(She did. It made a great difference later on.) I didn't let on about my birthday; what *could* I have been expecting?

The Gräfin, opening her letters over breakfast, gave a joyful cry and waved one over her head. It was the Baron's, re-forwarded several times! She read it out, and, on the strength of its splendid tenor, I thought of telling the truth about my Vienna improvisation but I didn't quite dare.

The day was dark and threatening. Why didn't I stay on a bit? How I would have liked to! But I was entangled in a fiction that no one believed and there was no way out. We were talking in the library, snugly surrounded by books, when the man in green announced that the car was waiting. No good saying, now, that I would rather walk to the station: I would have missed my unwanted train and been late for my phantom rendezvous ... But when we said goodbye, they looked truly worried, as though I were not quite safe on my own.

I sailed away, half-cocooned in a fur rug, in the back of an enormous car that swished its way, under an ever-darkening sky, to a little country station on the St Polten–Vienna line. A few warning flakes were falling when we arrived and the chauffeur jumped out, carrying my rucksack and stick. He wanted to help at the ticket office, put me into a corner seat and see me off.

Here was a new panic. Even had I wanted to go by train, I hadn't enough money for the ticket. All this brought on a recrudescence of last night's folly: someone had told me – *who, and where?* – that one tipped chauffeurs in Central Europe. Taking my stick and shouldering the rucksack, I found four coins in my pocket and pressed them on the chauffeur with mumbled thanks. He was a white-haired, friendly and cheerful old man, a former coachman, I think. He had been telling me, over his shoulder on the way, how he, too, had loved wandering about as a young man. He looked surprised and distressed at this sudden unwanted largesse – he didn't in the least expect me to try to keep up with the Liechtensteins – and he said, with real feeling, 'O nein, junger Herr!' and almost made as though to give the wretched coins back. Leaving him with his coroneted cap in his hand, scratching his head with a puzzled and unhappy look, I dashed in confusion into the station for cover and oblivion and watched him get slowly back in the car and drive off.

Few delights could compare with these wintry days: the snow outside, the bare trees outlined by the frost, the muted light and, indoors, the rooms following each other filled with the spoils, the heirlooms and the dowries of a golden age. The galleries of the hibernating city retreated and grew smaller in the distance, like vistas along dim rectangular telescopes. I had heard someone say that Vienna combined the splendour of a capital with the familiarity of a village. In the inner city, where crooked lanes opened on gold and marble outbursts of Baroque, it was true; and, in the Kärntnerstrasse or the Graben, after I had bumped into three brand-new acquaintances within a quarter of an hour, it seemed truer still and parts of the town suggested an even narrower focus. There were squares as small and complete and as carefully furnished as rooms. Façades of broken pediment and tiered shutter enclosed hushed rectangles of cobble; the drip of icicles eroded gaps in the frozen scallops of the fountains; the statues of archdukes or composers presided with pensive nonchalance; and all at once, as I loitered there, the silence would fly in pieces when the initial clang from a tower routed a hundred pigeons crowding a Palladian cornice and scattered avalanches of snow and filled the geometric sky with wings. Palace succeeded palace, casemented arches sailed across the streets, pillars lifted their statues; ice-fettered in their pools, tritons floundered beneath a cloudy heaven and ribbed cupolas expanded by the score. The greatest of these, the dome of the Karlskirche, floated with a balloon's lightness in an enclosing hemisphere of snow and the friezes that spiralled the shafts of the two statue-crowned guardian columns – free-standing and as heavily wrought as Trajan's – gained an added impromptu spin when they vanished halfway up in a gyre of flakes.

The American Bill Bryson has become one of the most popular travel writers of our time. The following is an extract from his *African Diary*.

Extract from *African Diary*

In the early evening we made our way to the modestly grand central railway station in Nairobi to catch the overnight sleeper to Mombasa. Kenya Railways has something of a tradition of killing its passengers. In just the past decade, a little over 200 people have died in accidents on its trains. The accident that seems to have attracted the most publicity in recent years was one in 1999 when the overnight Nairobi-to-Mombasa train jumped the rails at an interesting-sounding place called 'Man Eaters' Junction', in Tsavo National Park, killing 32 people.

The crew blamed brake failure. Kenya Railways blamed the crew. No one really knows what happened. The following year another thirty-plus people were killed in two accidents, both involving runaway trains, in the space of four days. The biggest disaster of all was in 1993, when a train bound for Mombasa from Nairobi plunged off a bridge and into the 'crocodile-infested' Ngai Ndeithya River, killing 140 people. *Ngai Ndeithya* means 'God help us' in Kiswahili, which would seem to be a not inappropriate motto for the railway itself. Almost since the beginning, however, the train has been known as the Lunatic Express. Can't think why.

Man Eaters' Junction is so called, by the way, because in 1898, during the construction of the railway, about 140 Indian workers were snatched and eaten by two lions (giving a whole new meaning to the term 'Indian takeaway'). The railway's chief engineer, an ex-army man named Lt. Col. John H. Patterson, spent months trying to lure the lions into a trap (often using understandably reluctant Indians as bait), but always failed. On one notable occasion a junior employee named C. H. Ryall sat up all night in an open railway carriage with a rifle trained on a pile of bait outside, but, unfortunately, nodded off. The lions ignored the bait and took poor Ryall instead.

Finally, in early December, after nine months of frustration, Patterson managed to bag one of the lions. Three weeks later, he shot and wounded the second one, which then bounded off into the bush. At first light the next morning, he followed the trail of blood to the beast's lair.

Though severely wounded, the lion charged. Patterson fired both barrels of his gun, and was nonplussed, to say the least, to find that the lion merely staggered sideways and then resumed coming for him. Turning to his rifle bearer for his backup gun, Patterson was additionally nonplussed to discover that the bearer was 50 feet away and climbing a tree. Patterson did likewise, just managing to haul himself onto a branch, the lion snapping at his quivering flanks. There, he snatched the gun from the cowering bearer and fired once more, and the lion at last fell dead. The fate of the bearer is not recorded, but I believe we may reasonably assume that he was not further entrusted with the custody of firearms.

The journey from Nairobi to Mombasa takes thirteen hours, nearly all of it after dark, which is perhaps a mercy, all things considered. So long as it stays upright and settled on the rails, the train is quite wonderful. It was a little on the ancient side, to be sure, but we each had a snug, private cabin, which looked comfortable enough, and the dining car was splendid, with a hearty three-course dinner and cheery, attentive service. Knowing the perils that lay ahead, we took the sensible precaution of anaesthetising ourselves with many Tusker beers before, during and after dinner, but even so, sleep was not to be found.

Another journey is described in *Journey to the Centre of the Earth* by Jules Verne. This is a very early, but still exciting, example of what we would now call 'Science Fiction':

Extract from *Journey to the Centre of the Earth*

The Great Explosion and the Rush Down Below

The next day, Thursday, August 27, is a well-remembered date in our subterranean journey. It never returns to my memory without sending through me a shudder of horror and palpitation of the heart. From that hour we had no further occasion for the exercise of reason, or judgement, or skill, or contrivance. We were henceforth to be hurled along, the playthings of the fierce elements of the deep.

At six we were afoot. The moment drew near to clear a way by blasting through the opposing mass of granite.

I begged for the honour of lighting the fuse. This duty done, I was to join my companions on the raft, which had not yet been unloaded; we should then push off as far as we could and avoid the dangers arising from the explosion.

The fuse was calculated to burn ten minutes before setting fire to the mine. I therefore had sufficient time to get away to the raft.

After a hasty meal, my uncle and the hunter embarked whilst I remained on shore. I was supplied with a lighted lantern to set fire to the fuse.

'Now go,' said my uncle, 'and return immediately.'

I immediately proceeded to the mouth of the tunnel. I opened my lantern. I laid hold of the end of the match.

The Professor stood, chronometer in hand.

'Ready?' he cried.

'Ay.'

'Fire!'

I instantly plunged the end of the fuse into the lantern.

It spluttered and flamed, and I ran at the top of my speed to the raft.

Hans, with a vigorous thrust, sent us from the shore. The raft shot twenty yards out to sea.

It was a moment of intense excitement. The Professor was watching the hand of the chronometer.

'Five minutes more!' he said. 'Four! Three!' My pulse beat half-seconds.

'Two! One! Down, granite rocks; down with you.'

What took place at that moment? I believe I did not hear the dull roar of the explosion. But the rocks suddenly assumed a new arrangement: they rent asunder like a curtain. I saw a bottomless pit open on the shore. The sea, lashed into sudden fury, rose up in an enormous billow, on the ridge of which the unhappy raft was uplifted bodily in the air with all its crew and cargo.

We all three fell down flat. In less than a second we were in deep, unfathomable darkness. Then I felt as if not only myself but the raft also had no support beneath. I thought it was sinking; but it was not so. I wanted to speak to my uncle, but the roaring of the waves prevented him from hearing even the sound of my voice.

In spite of darkness, noise, astonishment and terror, I then understood what had taken place.

On the other side of the blown-up rock was an abyss. The explosion had caused a kind of earthquake in this fissured and abysmal region; a great gulf had opened; and the sea, now changed into a torrent, was hurrying us along into it.

I gave myself up for lost.

The short story is often an excellent source for oral interpretation: many are broadcast on radio and the short story remains a popular genre for writers in English. The following extract is taken from *The Grave by the Handpost* by Thomas Hardy and it contains many references to old Christmas customs that have survived in one form or another everywhere that Christmas is now celebrated:

Extract from *The Grave by the Handpost*

I never pass through Chalk-Newton without turning to regard the neighbouring upland, at a point where a lane crosses the lone, straight highway dividing this from the next parish; a sight which does not fail to recall the event that once happened there; and, though it may seem superfluous, at this date, to disinter more memories of village history, the whispers of that spot may claim to be preserved.

It was a dark, yet mild and exceptionally dry evening at Christmas-time (according to the testimony of William Dewy of Mellstock, Michael Mail and others), that the choir of Chalk-Newton – large parish situated about halfway between the towns of Ivell and Casterbridge, and now a railway station – left their homes just before midnight to repeat their annual harmonies under the windows of the local population. The band of instrumentalists and singers was one of the largest in the country; and, unlike the smaller and finer Mellstock string band, which eschewed all but the catgut, it included brass and reed performers at full Sunday services and reached all across the west gallery.

On this night there were two or three violins, two 'cellos, a tenor viol[1], double bass, hautboy[2], clarionets, serpent[3], and seven singers. It was, however, not the choir's labours, but what its members chanced to witness that particularly marked the occasion.

They had pursued their rounds for many years without meeting with any incident of an unusual kind, but tonight, according to the assertions of several, there prevailed, to begin with, an exceptionally solemn and thoughtful mood among two or three of the oldest in the band, as if they were thinking they might be joined by the phantoms of dead friends who had been of their number in earlier years, and now were mute in the churchyard under flattening mounds – friends who had shown greater zest for melody in their time than was shown in this; or that some past voice of a semi-transparent figure might quaver from some bedroom-window its acknowledgement of their nocturnal greeting, instead of a familiar living neighbour. Whether this were fact or fancy, the younger members of the choir met together with their customary thoughtlessness and buoyancy. When they had gathered by the stone stump of the cross in the middle of the village, near the White Horse Inn, which they made their starting point, someone observed that they were full early, that it was not yet twelve o'clock. The local waits[4] of those days mostly refrained from sounding a note before Christmas morning had astronomically arrived, and not caring to return to their beer, they decided to begin with some outlying cottages in Sidlinch Lane, where the people had no clocks, and would not know whether it were night or morning. In that direction they accordingly went; and as they ascended to higher ground their attention was attracted by a light beyond the houses, quite at the top of the lane.

The road from Chalk-Newton to Broad Sidlinch is about two miles long and in the middle of its course, where it passes over the ridge dividing the two villages, it crosses at right angles, as has been stated, the lonely, monotonous, old highway known as Long Ash Lane, which runs, straight as a surveyor's line, many miles north and south of this spot, on the foundation of a Roman road, and has often been mentioned in these narratives. Though now quite deserted and grass-grown, at the beginning of the century it was well kept and frequented by traffic. The glimmering light appeared to come from the precise point where the roads intersected.

'I think I know what that did mean!' one of the group remarked.

They stood a few moments, discussing the probability of the light having origin in an event of which rumours had reached them, and resolved to go up the hill.

Notes:

1   the viol was six-stringed, the violin four-stringed

2   oboe

3   a cross between a cornet and a bugle. Its length of around eight feet meant it had to be shaped in a series of sharp curves, making it look rather like a serpent wriggling along the ground.

4   any band of musicians touring a district, rural or urban, singing carols, usually for reward.

A contemporary novelist once said that 'writing today you were always aware of the great mountain range of the nineteenth-century novel'. Some of the great peaks in that range are the novels by the Brontë sisters, Emily, Ann and Charlotte. Here is an extract from *Wuthering Heights* by Emily, which, like many of the 'Brontë' novels, has also been made into a movie and stage play:

Extract from *Wuthering Heights*

The narrator of the story, Mr Lockwood, makes his first visit to Wuthering Heights, the house set high on the moors:

The snow began to drive thickly. I seized the handle to essay another trial; when a young man without coat, and shouldering a pitchfork, appeared in the yard behind. He hailed me to follow him, and, after marching through a washhouse and a paved area containing a coal-shed, pump, and pigeon-cot, we at length arrived in the huge, warm cheerful apartment, where I was formerly received. It glowed delightfully in the radiance of an immense fire, compounded of coal, peat and wood; and near the table, laid for a plentiful evening meal, I was pleased to observe the "missis", an individual whose existence I had never previously suspected. I bowed and waited, thinking she would bid me take a seat. She looked at me, leaning back in her chair, and remained motionless and mute.

'Rough weather!' I remarked. 'I'm afraid, Mrs Heathcliff, the door must bear the consequence of your servants' leisure attendance: I had hard work to make them hear me.'

She never opened her mouth. I stared – she stared also: at any rate, she kept her eyes on me in a cool, regardless manner, exceedingly embarrassing and disagreeable.

'Sit down,' said the young man gruffly. 'He'll be in soon.'

I obeyed; and hemmed, and called the villain Juno, who deigned, at this second interview, to move the extreme tip of her tail, in token of owning my acquaintance.

'A beautiful animal!' I commented again. 'Do you intend parting with the little ones, madam?'

'They are not mine,' said the amiable hostess, more repellingly than Heathcliff himself could have replied.

'Ah, your favourites are among these?' I continued, turning to an obscure cushion full of something like cats.

'A strange choice of favourites!' she observed scornfully.

Unluckily, it was a heap of dead rabbits. I hemmed once more, and drew closer to the hearth, repeating my comment on the wildness of the evening.

'You should not have come out,' she said, rising and reaching from the chimney piece two of the painted canisters.

Her position before was sheltered from the light; now, I had a distinct view of her whole figure and countenance. She was slender, and apparently scarcely past girlhood; an admirable form, and the most exquisite little face that I have ever had the pleasure of beholding; small features, very fair; flaxen ringlets, or rather golden, hanging loose on her delicate neck; and eyes, had they been agreeable in expression, that would have been irresistible: fortunately for my susceptible heart, the only sentiment they evinced hovered between scorn, and a kind of desperation, singularly unnatural to be detected there. The canisters were almost out of her reach; I make a motion to aid her; she turned upon me as a miser might turn if anyone attempted to assist him in counting his gold.

'I don't want your help,' she snapped; 'I can get them for myself.'

'I beg you pardon!' I hastened to reply.

'Were you asked to tea?' she demanded, tying an apron over her neat black frock, and standing with a spoonful of the leaf poised over the pot.

'I shall be glad to have a cup,' I answered.

'Were you asked?' she repeated.

'No,' I said, half smiling. 'You are the proper person to ask me.'

She flung the tea back, spoon and all, and resumed her chair in a pet; her forehead corrugated, and her red underlip pushed out, like a child's ready to cry.

The novel was not a nineteenth-century invention. The following extract is from Henry Fielding's *Tom Jones*: an exuberant narrative and one of the first great novels in English:

Extract from *Tom Jones*

Chapter II

A short description of Squire Allworthy, and a fuller account of Miss Bridget Allworthy, his sister.

IN THAT PART of the western division of this kingdom which is commonly called Somersetshire, there lately lived and perhaps lives still, a gentleman whose name was Allworthy, and who might well be called the favourite of both nature and fortune; for both of these seem to have contended which should bless and enrich him most. In this contention, nature may seem to some to have come off victorious, as she bestowed on him many gifts, while fortune had only one gift in her power; but in pouring forth this, she was so very profuse, that others perhaps may think this single endowment to have been more than equivalent to all the various blessings which he enjoyed from nature. From the former of these he derived an agreeable person, a sound constitution, a sane understanding, and a benevolent heart; by the latter, he was decreed to the inheritance of one of the largest estates in the county.

This gentleman had in his youth married a very worthy and beautiful woman, of whom he had been extremely fond. By her he had three children, all of whom died in their infancy. He had likewise had the misfortune of burying this beloved wife herself, about five years before the time in which this history chooses to set out. This loss, however great, he bore like a man of sense and constancy, though it must be confessed he would often talk a little whimsically on this head; for he sometimes said he looked on himself as still married, and considered his wife as only gone a little before him, a journey which he should most certainly, sooner or later, take after her; and that he had not the least doubt of meeting her again in a place where he should never part with her more – sentiments for which his sense was arraigned by one part of his neighbours, his religion by a second, and his sincerity by a third.

He now lived, for the most part, retired in the country, with one sister, for whom he had a very tender affection. This lady was now somewhat past the age of thirty, an era at which, in the opinion of the malicious, the title of 'old maid' may with no impropriety be assumed. She was of that species of women whom you commend rather for good qualities than beauty, and who are generally called, by their own sex, very good sort of women – as good a sort of woman, madam, as you wish to know. Indeed, she was so far from regretting want of beauty, that she never mentioned that perfection, if it can be called one, without contempt; and would often thank God she was not as handsome as Miss Such-a-one, whom perhaps beauty had led into errors, which she might have otherwise avoided. Miss Bridget Allworthy (for that was the name of this lady) very rightly conceived the charms of person in a woman to be no better than snares for herself, as well as for others; and yet so discreet was she in her conduct, that her prudence was as much on the guard as if she had all the snares to apprehend which were ever laid for her whole sex. Indeed, I have observed, though it may seem unaccountable to the reader, that this guard of prudence, like the trained bands, is always readiest to go on duty where there is the least danger. It often basely and cowardly deserts those paragons for whom the men are all wishing, sighing, dying and spreading every net in their power; and constantly attends at the heels of that higher order of women for whom the other sex have a more distant and awful respect and whom (from despair, I suppose, of success) they never venture to attack.

Purely 'narrative prose' confines itself to telling a story and the 'voice' behind it is anonymous and totally unobtrusive. The following is an example of such informative writing that confines itself to a simple narrative. It is the summary of the action of a play that is, in itself, an adaptation of a poem. You might like to use this next extract as an example if you are asked to summarise the action of a play or a novel:

Extract from *Troilus and Criseyde*
(Adapted from Chaucer for the stage by Michael Herzog and Ken Pickering.)

SYNOPSIS

Troilus, the great Trojan warrior, claims to be immune from the power of Love until he sees the beautiful widow Criseyde at prayer. He becomes distraught and eventually reveals the cause to his friend Pandarus, who is Criseyde's uncle.

Pandarus offers to act as go-between and to instruct Troilus in love. Pandarus now visits Criseyde and tells her of what he knows. After her initial panic, Criseyde agrees to show some affection for Troilus, provided that no commitment is required of her. The scheming Pandarus creates a situation in which Criseyde visits Pandarus in his sickbed and the seeds of mutual affection are sown. Guiding him all the way, Pandarus now arranges for Troilus to come to Criseyde's bed and, after almost literally pushing him between the sheets, leaves Troilus to discover passion.

Just as it seems that the two lovers have found total contentment, Fortune turns her wheel, and Criseyde is forced to leave Troilus as a hostage to the Greeks in an exchange. Troilus is heartbroken, but Criseyde assures him that she will find a way to return and promises to do so in ten days.

Time passes and Criseyde does not return. Eventually, the unhappy Troilus, after an exchange of letters with his love, discovers proof of her infidelity with a Greek warrior.

Troilus dies in battle and views the scene of his unhappiness from heaven, whereas Pandarus is left to explain his manipulations and remind the audience of the perils of the love game.

There are three characters and the play requires a single, multi-focus setting. There is a series of beautiful songs for both Troilus and Criseyde.

A great deal of prose writing is concerned with persuasion or with presenting an argument. The following speech was originally made as a radio broadcast by Lilian Baylis, who grew up in South Africa. Lilian went to London in the early years of the twentieth century and was responsible for the success of the famous Old Vic Theatre, with its policy of presenting all of Shakespeare's plays for 'everyone', including thousands of school pupils. This speech was included in the play *Monday Nights Have Got to be Better* by Anthea Preston, so it could be used as an acting piece:

Extract from *Monday Nights Have Got to be Better*

'I so believe the theatre is our greatest power for good or evil, that I pray my earnestness may give me words in which to express this faith and hold your attention ... I am cast tonight to speak on the Art of Living and the place of theatre in that life. The theatre isn't an excuse for wonderful evening gowns and jewels; it isn't a fad of people with long hair and sandals or the perquisite of varsity men and women; it is a crying need of working men and women who need to see beyond the four walls of their offices into a world of awe and wonder. Furthermore, all art is a bond between rich and poor; it allows of no class distinction;

and it is a bond between nation and nation. Dr Dearmer said: "Art is a spiritual necessity. Civilisation cannot exist in its absence, for without it, civilisation is but organised savagery". The theatre is perhaps the most important and accessible and the most easily understood branch of art for the man and woman in the street.'

The seventeenth-century poet and playwright John Dryden presents an interesting argument on the nature of drama and acting in his *Essay on Dramatic Poetry*. Once you have mastered the writer's line of thinking and some of the archaic language, you will find this a powerful piece of persuasive writing and speaking:

Extract from *Essay on Dramatic Poetry*

THE USE OF DESCRIPTION IN DRAMA

I HAVE observed that in all our tragedies, the audience cannot forbear laughing when the actors are to die; it is the most comic part of the whole play. All *passions* may be lively represented on the stage, if to the well-writing of them the actor supplies a good commanded voice, and limbs that move easily, and without stiffness; but there are many *actions* which can never be imitated to a just height: dying especially is a thing which none but a Roman gladiator could naturally perform on the stage, when he did not imitate or represent, but do it; and therefore it is better to omit the representation of it.

The words of a good writer which describe it lively, will make a deeper impression of belief in us than all the actor can insinuate into us, when he seems to fall dead before us; as a poet in the description of a beautiful garden, or a meadow, will please our imagination more than the place itself can please our sight. When we see death represented, we are convinced it is but fiction; but when we hear it related, our eyes, the strongest witnesses, are wanting, which might have undeceived us; and we are all willing to favour the sleight when the poet does not too grossly impose on us. They, therefore, who imagine these relations, would make no concernment in the audience are deceived, by confounding them with the other, which are of things antecedent to the play: those are made often in cold blood, as I may say, to the audience; but these are warmed with our concernments, which were before awakened in the play. What the philosophers say of motion, that, when it is once begun, it continues of itself and will do so to eternity without some stop put to it, is clearly true on this occasion: the soul being already moved with the characters and fortunes of those imaginary persons, continues going of its own accord; and we are no more weary to hear what becomes of them when they are not on the stage, than we are to listen to the news of an absent mistress. But it is objected, that if one part of the play may be related, then why not all? I answer, some parts of the action are more fit to be represented, some to be related.

Advanced Poetry:

This collection of verse includes the complexity, sophistication and richness of form, language and ideas appropriate for performance at an advanced level. The poems are widely varied in style and content, but they all present challenging emotions, passions, narratives and beliefs. They range from love poems to outbursts of rage and indignation: some come from parts of the world where conflict is a part of everyday life and others deal with romantic ideas and ancient legends. The majority of the poems are by living and modern writers, although there are also wonderful pieces from earlier writings in English.

The poems are categorised as *narrative* or *lyric*. These can be slippery definitions, but where the 'voice' of the writer is simply reporting or describing without revealing an emotional or ideological position, we have designated them *narrative* poems. Some poems in the *lyric* section may appear to cross the boundary into *narrative* and vice versa, and that can provide lively material for discussion. The *narrative* section continues our concern with storytelling, but you should remember that there is also a story behind every *lyric* poem to be shared with the listener.

Narrative Poems:

The simple ballad form of this next poem evokes a mysterious and haunting story:

La Belle Dame Sans Merci by John Keats (England)

Oh what can ail thee, knight-at-arms,
Alone and palely loitering?
The sedge has withered from the lake,
And no birds sing.

'Oh what can ail thee, knight-at-arms,
So haggard and so woe-begone?
The squirrel's granary is full,
And the harvest's done.

'I see a lily on thy brow
With anguish moist and fever dew,
And on they cheeks a fading rose
Fast withereth too.'

I met a lady in the meads,
Full beautiful – a faery's child,
Her hair was long, her foot was light,
And her eyes were wild.

I made a garland for her head,
And bracelets too, and fragrant zone,
She looked at me as she did love,
And made sweet moan.

I set her on my pacing steed,
And nothing else saw all day long,
For sidelong would she bend, and sing
A faery's song.

She found me roots of relish sweet,
And honey wild, and manna dew,
And sure in language strange she said –
'I love thee true!'

She took me to her elfin grot,
And there she wept and sighed full sore,
And there I shut her wild, wild eyes
With kisses four.

And there she lulled me asleep,
And there I dreamed – ah! woe betide!
The latest dream I ever dreamed
On the cold hill's side.

I saw pale kings and princes too,
Pale warriors, death-pale were they all;
They cried –'La Belle Dame sans Merci
Hath thee in thrall!'

I saw their starved lips in the gloam,
With horrid warning gaped wide,
And I awoke and found me here,
On the cold hill's side.

And this is why I sojourn here,
Alone and palely loitering,
Though the sedge is withered from the lake,
And no birds sing.

Work and working conditions have often inspired narrative ballads. This next poem derives its story from the early mining community in the USA:

Flynn of Virginia by **Bret Harte**

Didn't know Flynn –
Flynn of Virginia –
Long as he's been 'yar?
Look 'ee here, stranger,
Whar hev you been?

Here in this tunnel
He was my pardner,
That same Tom Flynn –
Working together,
In wind and weather,
Day out and in.

Didn't know Flynn!
Well, that is queer.
Why, it's a sin
To think of Tom Flynn –
Tom, with his cheer,
Tom, without fear –
Stranger, look 'yar!

Thar in the drift,
Back to the wall,
He held the timbers
Ready to fall;
Then in the darkness
I heard him call:

'Run for your life, Jake!
Run for your wife's sake!
Don't wait for me.'
And that was all
Heard in the din,
Heard of Tom Flynn –
Flynn of Virginia.

The Scottish poet Thomas Campbell used the ancient, traditional ballad form to tell a gripping story. Here is his poem followed by a traditional Scottish ballad that Campbell was imitating:

Lord Ullin's Daughter by **Thomas Campbell**

A chieftain to the Highlands bound
Cries 'Boatman, do not tarry!
And I'll give thee a silver pound
To row us o'er the ferry!'

'Now who be ye, would cross Lochgyle
This dark and stormy water?'
'O I'm the chief of Ulva's isle,
And this, Lord Ullin's daughter.'

'And fast before her father's men
Three days we've fled together,
For should he find us in the glen,
My blood would stain the heather.'

'His horsemen hard behind us ride –
Should they our steps discover,
Then who will cheer my bonny bride
When they have slain her lover?'

Out spoke the hardy Highland wight,
'I'll go, my chief, I'm ready:
It is not for your silver bright,
But for your winsome lady:'

'And by my word! the bonny bird
In danger shall not tarry;
So though the waves are raging white
I'll row you o'er the ferry.'

By this the storm grew loud apace,
The water-wraith was shrieking;
And in the scowl of heaven each face
Grew dark as they were speaking.

But still as wilder blew the wind
And as the night grew drearer,
Adown the glen rode armed men,
Their trampling sounded nearer.

'O haste thee, haste!' the lady cries,
'Though tempests round us gather;
I'll meet the raging of the skies,
But not an angry father.'

The boat has left a stormy land,
A stormy sea before her, –
When, O! too strong for human hand
The tempest gather'd o'er her.

And still they row'd amidst the roar
Of waters fast prevailing:
Lord Ullin reach'd that fatal shore, –
His wrath was changed to wailing.

For, sore dismay'd, through storm and shade
His child he did discover:-
One lovely hand she stretch'd for aid,
And one was round her lover.

'Come back! Come back!' he cried in grief
'Across this stormy water:
And I'll forgive your Highland chief,
My daughter! – O my daughter!'

'Twas vain: the loud waves lash'd the shore,
Return or aid preventing:
The waters wild went o'er his child,
And he was left lamenting.

The Douglas Tragedy **Traditional anon.**

'Rise up, rise up, Lord Douglas!' she says,
'And put on your armour so bright;
Let it ne'er be said that a daughter of ours
Was married to a lord under night.

'Rise up, rise up, my seven bold sons,
And put on your armour so bright;
And take better care o' your youngest sister,
For your eldest's away this night!'

Lady Margaret was on a milk-white steed,
Lord William was on a gray,
A buglet-horn hung down by his side,
And swiftly they rode away.

Lord William looked over his left shoulder
To see what he could see,
And there he spied her seven bold brothers,
Come riding over the lea.

'Light down, light down, Lady Margaret,' he said,
'And hold my steed in your hand,
Until that against your seven bold brothers,
And your father, I make a stand.'

O there she stood, and bitter she stood,
And never shed one tear,
Until she saw her brothers fa',
And her father who loved her so dear.

'O hold your hand, Lord William!' she said,
'For your strokes are deep and sore;
Though lovers I can get many a one,
A father I can never get more.'

O she's taken off her handkerchief,
It was o' the holland so fine,
And aye she dressed her father's wounds;
His blood ran down like wine.

'O choose, O choose, Lady Margaret,
Will ye go with me, or bide?'
'I'll go, I'll go, Lord William,' she said.
'Ye've left me no other guide.'

He lifted her up on her milk-white steed,
And mounted his dapple-gray,
With his buglet-horn hung down by his side,
And slowly they rode away.

O they rode on, and on they rode,
And a' by the light o' the moon,
Until they came to a wan water,
And there lighted down.

They lighted down to take a drink
O the spring that ran so clear,
But down the stream ran his red heart's blood;
And she began to fear.

'Hold up, hold up, Lord William,' she said,
'I fear me you are slain!'
''Tis but the shadow o' my scarlet cloak
That shines in the water so plain.'

O they rode on, and on they rode,
And a' by the light o' the moon,
Until they saw his mother's ha',
And there they lighted down.

'Get up, get up, lady mother,' he says,
'Get up, and let in your son!
Open the door, lady mother,' he says,
'For this night my fair lady I've won!

'Now make my bed, lady mother,' he says,
'O make it wide and deep,
And lay Lady Margaret close at my back,
And the sounder will I sleep!'

Lord William was dead long ere midnight,
Lady Margaret long ere day,
And all true lovers that go together
May they have more luck than they!

Lord William was buried in Mary's Kirk,
Lady Margaret in Mary's Quire;
And out of her grave grew a bonny red rose,
And out of the knight's a brier.

The contemporary British poet John Wright has recently performed some of his poetry at the world-famous 'Oyster Festival' in the fishing town of Whitstable. Here is one of his ironic comments on the modern world that is obviously written for performance:

Short Term Tenants by John Wright

An unusual couple came to live next
Door in the wee black cottage whose odd
Front door stays tightly closed from the racing
Road (a flimsy barrier from the Senna
Mimic – the speed-sotted driver whose trademark
Gimmick is to slice the bend at sixty
Five, mocking the gods that he'll make it –
Alive – leaving in shreds the thirty mile
Limit).

They entered and went past the small garden
Hut through a door at the side, usually
Shut but which suited their purposes
Very well: he, early starting, sometimes
Home late; she, there most days then gone, left him
To wait her return with a parcel of
Fish – from the Shetland Isles! (She'd said she'd a
Wish to go back there to live) to offer
Her mate.

He was far gone on cooking. Made him feel
Good: those curries and spices; all that fresh
Food; exotic aromas; simmering
Pans. Was she his assistant? I never
Knew. More like, she reclined with a leisurely
Brew to muse on a life in far away
Isles, and abandon herself to his culinary
Wiles; undone later on by his poisson
Ragout.

I learned he was expert in all things I
T. Held down a smart job though never felt
Free to follow his heart. Was struggling each
Day to keep up the pace, digesting all
Trends that the journals revealed; making
Amends as well as he could when failing
To keep nose ahead in the race: mortgaged
His sleep even, hardly went out even seldom made
Friends.

It all got too much; they decided to
Leave. Escape to the Shetlands. They seemed to
Believe they would find their nirvana up
There with the winds and the wild winter
Days. She'd teach a small class. They'd welcome her
Ways, her bone china accent, her neat, discrete
Dress. He'd work through the 'net, get paid rather
Less, but hone up his skills as an amateur
Chef.

One of the joys of compiling and perusing an anthology is in finding previously unknown writers. Here is the first of a number of poems by Winifred Mustoe that will reward study and performance. It may remind you of the poem *Adlestrop* by Edward Thomas, and is therefore a good example of what scholars call 'intertextuality':

Wayside Station by **Winifred Mustoe**

They crowd the platform, these old-fashioned flowers –
Snapdragons, asters, hollyhocks – all bright
With memories of some long-vanished childhood
When scents and colours set the world alight.
No-one has left the train, no-one has entered.
Cradled in summer's warmth and peace, the place
Pulls like a glimpse of some long-lost Atlantis,
Touches my spirit with a kind of grace.

And now the impulse grows – to break my journey
For days, for weeks, for ever; to remain
In this quiet spot whose air seems full of healing,
Whose smiling welcome would dissolve my pain;
Whose beauty would walk through the years behind me;
Whose gentleness might teach me to forget
Fears of the years ahead. The impulse strengthens,
And then a voice within: 'Not here – not yet.'

The train prepares to leave. The lost Atlantis,
Submerged by distance, disappears from view.
The miles flash by. I have no means of testing
If all or any of my thoughts were true.
Distance is relative. No seasoned traveller,
I journey seldom – choose the known and near,
But far – too far – through lands of lost illusions
To break my journey here.

At this level, all students should begin to take responsibility for their own learning and not rely solely on a teacher or tutor. This next poem is a powerful reminder of that fact from the Hong Kong poet Gillian Bickley:

Graduation by **Gillian Bickley**

Will you write something about all of us?
the tall student shyly asks, self-deprecatingly.

– What is there to say?

That you sat in front of me for fourteen weeks,
did the assignments I requested,
spoke up when I asked you to
and bravely took the floor, when it was your turn.

You did what was required.

Some of you asked me what to think,
and a very few,
agreeing,
when I said,
'Think for yourselves',
dared to
disagree with me.

Some of you thought me
unreasonable, to expect you to read
the few books set,

feeling
my more proper behaviour
was, to give you
handouts, model essays,
which would
indirectly
tip you off
what the examination questions
would be,
and do them for you.

Some of you found some enlightenment
in the foreign books I put before you, new ideas
that resonated with your personal growth.
Some of you were startled and surprised to find in foreign
lives so many social issues like your own.

You are very different
from the Hong Kong students of the
seventies, burnt and burning from the Cultural Revolution;
from the students of the eighties,
wondering what
Hong Kong under Chinese rule would be
and weeping for lost friends at Tienamen.

You have arrived at another place,
political and personal maturity
in a modern society

and are planning
responsibly to make it yours.

I wish you luck!

A simple event is given profound significance in this next poem from India:

Night of the Scorpion by Nissim Ezekiel

I remember the night my mother
was stung by a scorpion. Ten hours
of steady rain had driven him
to crawl beneath a sack of rice.
Parting with his poison – flash
of diabolic tail in the dark room –
he risked the rain again.
The peasants came like swarms of flies
and buzzed the Name of God a hundred times
to paralyse the Evil One.
With candles and with lanterns
throwing giant scorpion shadows
on the mud-baked walls
they search for him: he was not found.
They clicked their tongues.

With every movement that the scorpion made
his poison moved in mother's blood, they said.
May he sit still, they said.
May the sins of your previous birth
be burned away tonight, they said.
May your suffering decrease
the misfortunes of your next birth, they said.
May the sum of evil
balanced in this unreal world
against the sum of good
become diminished by your pain.

May the poison purify your flesh
of desire, and your spirit of ambition,
they said, and they sat around
on the floor with my mother in the centre,
the peace of understanding on each face.

More candles, more lanterns, more neighbours,
more insects, and the endless rain.
My mother twisted through and through
groaning on a mat.
My father, sceptic, rationalist,
trying every curse and blessing,
powder, mixture, herb and hybrid.
He even poured a little paraffin
upon the bitten toe and put a match to it.
I watched the flame feeding on my mother.
I watched the holy man perform his rites
to tame the poison with an incantation.
After twenty hours
it lost its sting.

My mother only said
Thank God the scorpion picked on me
and spared my children.

The following is one of several impressive poems from winners of the recent STSD poetry competition:

Love in Darkness by Joan Goodall

She left him long ago yet he can hear
staccato steps, stiletto heeled so near
He's sure she's there and soon, so soon a strand
of her red hair will touch his face, her hand
with mothlike lightness brush away a tear.

Four nights ago her image was so clear
he spoke her name but she did not appear
In morning light. Preferring night she planned
to be with him in darkness.

He lives molelike in darkness now for fear
she will not come and waits for night, each ear
alert for step or breath, her slightest sound.
He shuns the light and cannot understand
why once he loved the sun for now she's here
to be with him in darkness.

The following poem reminds us of the world that we have created for the next generation and might sting us into indignation – extract from *Poetry for Palestine*:

The Back Step by Annette al-Habib

Toy tanks lined up in the dirt near the back step,
Pushed and pulled by dimpled, chubby, grubby, baby hands,
While inside his golden, curly little head
He creates his dreams of battles in far off foreign lands.
And clear blue eyes see endless apple blossom by the garden wall.

A soldier now sits upon the step, and watches through the summer haze
The blood of comrades making mud and dust,
While screams split the air and mines explode inside his brain,
And the wireless tells of certain victory and a cause that's just.
And tired, red, eyes envy the blackbird, safe on his leafy perch.

And now, in middle age, the scene is still the same.
The back step feels harder as he listens to the football game.
Pot-bellied, balding, successful to no small degree,
Half-time. Satellite news, Ireland, Bosnia. How many refugees?
While evening wood-smoke rises through the golden apple tree.

A patio, with slabs, adorns the area at the back.
A chair is carefully placed, and granddad sits, all neatly wrapped
Against the crispness of the morning air,
And a little boy with golden hair
Plays war games at his feet
And listens to tales of victory and defeat,
While unseen, the blackbird makes his silent retreat.

We are pleased to be publishing two poems by the important South African poet Trevor Whittock for the first time. They are another cry against injustice:

The Travellers by **Trevor Whittock** (Johannesburg)

Sitting together on a bench
In Joubert Park,
Grasping hands only,
They heard in the city dusk
A locomotive whistle.

Merging memories and desires
Woke to sensation
With that distant wailing:
Of strangers undressing
In the yellow light of a compartment,
Darkness of Karoo spaces outside,
Blurred rock rising to the window,
Falling back into darkness;
A wait at some dorp station
With a faint steam hiss
And Afrikaans half-heard
On the borders of sleep,
Till a whistle wails its reassurance,
And they cling together,
In the rhythmic heart
Of a voyaging train.

The Mannequins in Cape Town by **Trevor Whittock**

The mannequins pose
In the fluorescent windows,
One in a frock of pale rose,
One with a shawl of silver sequins.

The brunette smoothes the furls
Of her skirt,
The blonde
Pats her moulded curls.

And they stare through the curved glass
At the coloured men hosing the street,
And deafly smile at the coarse-coloured talk
For the pink lobes of their ears are wax.

They stare at the black stream
Swirling by with fluorescent reflections,
But they are blind,
And the pupils of their eyes
Are only wax studs in hollow circles.

Many of the poems included in this section are suitable for group performance, choral speaking or dramatisation. Now included is a dramatised version of one of R. H. Barham's *Ingoldsby Legends* that were as popular in their day as the works of Dickens. The poem may be spoken by a single voice (as it was originally written), or used in any way you wish. The setting for this story of smuggling and devilish magic is in an area off the south-east coast of England known as the Isle of Thanet:

The Smuggler's Leap by R. H. Barham

(Taken from *The Ingoldsby Legends* adapted for the stage by Ken Pickering and published by J. Garnet Miller Ltd.)

BARHAM The fire-flash shines from Reculver Cliff
   And the answering light burns blue in the skiff.
   And there they stand,
   That smuggling band,
   Some in the water and some on the sand.
SMUGGLER 1 Ready those contraband goods to land.
BARHAM The night is dark, they are silent and still.
BILL At the head of the party is Smuggler Bill!
   Now lower away! Come, lower away,
   We must be far, ere the dawn of the day.
   If Exciseman Gill should get scent of the prey
   And should come, and should catch us here,
   What would he say?

BARHAM The cargo's lowered from the dark skiff's side,

    And the tow line drags the tubs through the tide.

BILL Now mount, my merry men, mount and ride!

                               [*They mount horses and ride with kegs*

BARHAM Merrily now, in a goodly row,

    Away and away those smugglers go

    And they laugh at Exciseman Gill.

ALL Ho! Ho!

GILL [*suddenly appearing with his men*]

    When out from the turn, of the road to Herne

    Comes Gill, wide awake to the whole concern!

SMUGGLERS [*scattering in confusion. Each says one or more of the following*

    lines]

    Away, and away, and away they flew!

    Some dropping one tub, some dropping two.

    Some gallop this way, and some gallop that,

    Through Fordwich Level via Sandwich Flat,

    Those in a hurry make for Sturry.

OFFICERS With custom house officers close in their rear,

    Down Rushbourne Lane, and so by Westbere.

SMUGGLERS Away and away and away they flew!

    Some seek Whitstable, some Grove Ferry,

    Spurring and whipping like madmen-very

    For life!

GILL And Exciseman Gill,

    Sticks in pursuit of Smuggler Bill

WOMEN WATCHING THE CHASE

WOMAN 1 Smuggler Bill is six feet high,

    He has curling locks

WOMAN 2 And a roving eye.

WOMAN 3 He has a tongue and he has a smile

    Trained the female heart to beguile.

WOMAN 2 And there's not a farmer's wife in the Isle

From St Nicholas quite to the Foreland Light but

That eye and that tongue and that smile will wheedle her!

BILL Follow who will, ride after who may.

No one will catch my dapple grey.

Ho! Ho! Ho! Exciseman Gill

I draw out my flask and sip my fill! *[He does so*

BARHAM Down Chislett Lane so free and so fleet

Rides Smuggler Bill and away to Upstreet.

GILL [*losing ground in the distance*] I would give my soul

For a nag that would catch Smuggler Bill –

If I had but one! Bay or Dun.

DEVIL [*riding up beside him – disguised in a cap*] Done!

GILL Devil take me!

BARHAM Quoth Exciseman Gill.

GILL If I had but that horse, I'd have Smuggler Bill!

BARHAM He'd just uttered the words which I've mentioned to you

When his horse threw

Him head over heels and away he flew.

GILL [*raging and rolling*] I'd rather grill

Than not come up with that Smuggler Bill.

DEVIL Mount! Mount! On the back of my dun – you'll bother him yet.

I'll give you a lift – you're up on him – so.

He's a rum one to look at – a devil to go. *[He zooms off*

BARHAM Exciseman Gill dashed up the hill

And marked not, so eager was he in pursuit

The queer custom house officer's queer looking boot!

BILL [*aware of the other horse closing on him*] 'Tis my enemy again!

Now speed, now speed, my dapple grey steed

Thou ever, my dapple, went good in need.

O'er Monkton Mead, through Minster Level,

We'll baffle him yet – e'en be he the devil

For Manston Cave away, away!

Now speed thee, now speed thee, my good dapple grey.

It shall never be said that Smuggler Bill

Was run down like a hare by Exciseman Gill.

Manston Cave is my abode,

A mile to the north of the Ramsgate Road.

GILL Yield thee! Now yield thee, thou Smuggler Bill!

BARHAM Smuggler Bill looks behind

And sees a Dun horse come swift as the wind.

His nostrils smoke and his eyes they blaze.

Every shoe he has got appears red hot!

[Sparks and weird lights appear around GILL'*s horse*

BILL [*drawing his pistols*] I ne'er miss my aim. [*Huge bang*

VOICE From the dun horse there came not blood but flame!

[*GILL gets* BILL *by the scruff of the neck.*

Slow-motion action

The dapple grey mare made a desperate bound

Alas, alack on what dangerous ground.

Down the rugged sides so dreadfully steep

Where the chalk cave yawns full sixty feet deep

Down they went – O the terrible fall

Horses, Exciseman, Smuggler – all.

OLD WOMAN Down there I found as I walked around

All smashed and dashed, three mangled corpses –

Two of them human, the third was a horse's

I think it was that Exciseman Gill

Yet grasping the collar of Smuggler Bill.

But where was the other horse – from that

Terrible night he was seen by none.

BARHAM [*reappearing as himself to address the* AUDIENCE]

There are some people think, though I am not one,

That part of the story all nonsense and fun.

But Thanet folk there, one and all declare
That when the inquest considered the death of the pair
They heard a loud horse laugh up in the air!
If on one of those trips of the steamboat 'Eclipse'
You should go down to Margate to look at the ships –
Or take what bathing people call 'dips'
You may hear folks talk of that quarry of chalk
Or go over – it's rather far for a walk –
But a three-shilling drive will give you a peep
At that fearful chalk pit – so awfully deep
Which is called to this moment *The Smuggler's Leap*.

The ghosts of BILL *and* GILL *appear*

And it is said, on a moon-shining night,
If you look in that chalk pit white
You may see, if you will, the ghost of old Gill
Grappling the ghost of Smuggler Bill
And the ghost of the dapple grey lying between 'em
I'm told so, I can't say I know one who's seen 'em!

The following extract demonstrates how a contenporary poet uses the narrative form. This evocative poem is about the East Anglian port of Lowestoft.

The Iron Bridge by John Ward

Across the iron bridge there lie
the spiral streets that twist and dive
the corner ways and alleys blind
where if eyes and ears are opened up
the scenes and shows don't slow nor stop,
amongst these stones and brickwork lines
amongst these carbon-covered shops

amongst these scores and wrinkled lanes,
caught in countenance sublime
in fissured faces settled there
the age-etched maps of life and time.
These rocks and soil, sea and sand
shape the face behind the hand
that shapes the land and builds a town
that traps and holds them hard and bound
to trudge the streets and wear them down,
but the ghosts of stone store the steps
of the dead that walk this way,
the clammy cobbles worn and grey
the wooden doors and walls engraved
with graffiti ground like epitaphs
proclaiming love and stating hate,
sharp new scars and fading dates
across the town the red brick waits
the latest hands to carve the cry,
the ancient words, the oldest lines
Jimmy
      loves Ruth
           forever ...

Youth clubs and pubs,
the sweat shop night spots,
crammed with the jabber of couples' conversation and the
insistent monotone
bedroom beat of a drum box.
Locked in an embrace
Jimmy and Ruth's hearts race as they sway ungracefully across the
flashing floor.
Nothing more is needed

as the first flames of young love ignite in their hearts, heads
and loins,
consuming and then consummated

> later in the night ...

The orange lights gild the wet streets as they leave,
as the crowds on the corners tuck into takeaways and shout
loudly across the road.
The boys in their best white shirts,
the girls with their arms crossed across their chests
doing their bare best to keep warm in their black slit short skirts
and topple-high heels.
Jimmy's beery breath hangs in the air,
his jacket around Ruth's shoulders as she shudders in the one
o'clock shadows,
heading for home, surrounding one another.
He sez he 'lovesa' and she smiles,
hiding her head in his chest
as they walk awkwardly in a cold caress to a southside bedsit block.

> He stops.
> Fumbles and unlocks.
> She stumbles,
> > blindly in.

The anonymous numbers on the dirty doors
the stale food smell on every floor,
the echoing steps on the carpet-less stairs
the unwanted papers,
the onion air.

> Still, they scuttle and scuff and leave them there,
> complete the climb
> and close the door.

There, amongst the CD cases and coffee cups
on the floor,
watched by the posters
hung up
on the wall,
together,
on the sunken sofa,
they play the game.
>The talking,
>the tempting,
>the teasing and touching,
>the kissing and caressing.
>They make love ...
>A baby cries in the room above
and a fire truck passes
its rousing siren racing to dowse the flames
in some other part of town.
Jimmy and Ruth cool down,
their blaze burnt out,
leaving their hearts to hope,
>and the unspoken doubt

Lyric Poetry:

The first two poems in this section consider the nature of poetry itself
– the first is by the Hong Kong poet Gillian Bickley and the second by
the British actor, scriptwriter, poet and stand-up comic Henry Normal:

Welcome by **Gillian Bickley**

Writing poetry is a good way to communicate
in this busy world. In the interstices
of appointments, duties, transport connections
and pleasures,

memories recur
are dwelt on
interpreted, revised;
until one day
you make it known
that you would like to hear
something from me.

And there they are, waiting for me,
ready to be written down,
quite quickly,

and handed over to you
efficiently,

– the sweets and pills of my life
which you can swallow, absorb, or
pass-on – without giving them much of
your time

either.

Trust Me I'm a Poet by **Henry Normal**

Trust me
I'm a poet
    refining
      redefining
        revising
My business is Truth PLC

    enhancing
      enriching
        elaborating
Truth is my raw material
    My vocation
    My deity
    My mistress

    like a deft magician
    manipulating the imagery
correcting
correlating

concealing
I reveal the corruption of truth in tantalising
glimpses

    evoking the senses
      managing the facts
editing and selecting the words in my care
    omitting the irrelevant
      on your behalf

Trust me
I'm a poet
A doctor of truth

During the time of Shakespeare, many child actors were used in the London theatre – here is an epitaph to one of them by the playwright Ben Jonson:

CXX Epitaph on S.P., A Child of Q[ueen] EL[izabeth's] Chapel

Weep with me all you that read
This little story:
And know, for whom a tear you shed,
Death's self is sorry.
'Twas a child, that so did thrive
In grace, and feature,
As Heaven and Nature seemed to strive
Which owned the creature.
Years he numbered scarce thirteen
When Fates turned cruel,
Yet three filled zodiacs had he been
The stage's jewel;
And did act (what now we moan)
Old men so duly,
As, sooth, the Parcae thought him one,
He played so truly.
So, by error, to his fate
They all consented;
But viewing him since (alas, too late)
They have repented.
And have sought (to give new birth)
In baths to steep him;
But, being so much too good for earth,
Heaven vows to keep him.

The life of the sixteenth-century poet Sir Thomas Wyatt was almost a novel in itself. Lover of Ann Boleyn and twice imprisoned in the tower of London, he was partly responsible for introducing the sonnet into the English language and his poetry explores the depths of human emotions:

The Lover Showeth How he is Forsaken of Such as he Sometime Enjoyed by Sir Thomas Wyatt

They flee from me, that somtime did me seke
With naked fote stalkyng within my chamber.
Once have I seen them gentle, tame, and meke,
That now are wild, and do not once remember
That sometyme they have put them selves in danger,
To take bread at my hand, and now they range,
Busily sekyng in continuall change.
Thanked be fortune, it hath bene otherwise
Twenty tymes better: but one especiall,
In thinne array, after a pleasant gypse,
When her loose gowne did from her shoulders fall,
And she me caught in her armes long and small,
And therwithall, so swetely did me kysse,
And softly sayd: deare hart, how like you this?
It was no dreame: for I lay broade awakyng.
But all is turned now through my gentlenesse,
Into a bitter fashion of forsakying;
And I have leave to go of her goodnesse,
And she also to use newfanglenesse.
But, sins that I unkyndly so am served:
How like you this, what hath she now deserved?

The poems of the seventeenth-century poet Thomas Traherne were only discovered in manuscript by an antiquarian bookseller in the nineteenth century. There is a deceptive simplicity in the faith of this clergyman:

Wonder by **Thomas Traherne** (England, 1637–1674)

How like an angel came I down!
How bright are all things here!
When first among his works I did appear,
Oh, how their Glory me did crown!
The world resembled his Eternity,
In which my soul did walk;
And every thing that I did see
Did with me talk.

The skies in their magnificence,
The lively, lovely air;
Oh, how divine, how soft, how sweet, how fair!
The stars did entertain my sense,
And all the works of God so bright and pure,
So rich and great did seem
As if they ever must endure
In my esteem.

A native health and innocence
Within my bones did grow,
And while my God did all his glories show,
I felt a vigour in my sense
That was all spirit. I within did flow
With seas of life, like wine;
I nothing in the world did know,
But 'twas divine.

Harsh, ragged objects were concealed,
Oppressions, tears, and cries,
Sins, griefs, complaints, dissentions, weeping eyes,
Were hid: and only things revealed
Which heavenly spirits and the angels prize.
The State of Innocence
And Bliss, not trades and poverties,
Did fill my sense.

The streets were paved with golden stones,
The boys and girls were mine;
Oh, how did all their lovely faces shine!
The Sons of Men were Holy Ones,
Joy, Beauty, Welfare did appear to me,
And everything which here I found,
While like an angel I did see,
Adorned the ground.

Rich diamond, and pearl, and gold
In every place was seen;
Rare splendours, yellow, blue, red, white and green,
Mine eyes did everywhere behold;
Great Wonders clothed with Glory did appear,
Amazement was my Bliss.
That and my wealth was everywhere:
No Joy to this ...

The Welsh poet Dafydd ap Gwilym reveals a similar sense of rapture as he likens a day in spring to a religious event – the Mass:

May (The Woodland Mass) by Dafydd ap Gwilym

A pleasant place I was at today,
under mantles of the worthy green hazel,
listening at day's beginning
to the skilful cock thrush
singing a splendid stanza
of fluent signs and symbols;
a stranger here, wisdom his nature,
a brown messenger who had journeyed far,
coming from rich Carmarthenshire
at my golden girl's command.
About him was a setting
of flowers of the sweet boughs of May,
like green mantles, his chasuble
was of the wings of the wind.
There was here, by the great God,
nothing but gold in the altar's canopy.
I heard, in polished language,
a long and faultless chanting,
an unhesitant reading to the people
of a gospel without mumbling;
the elevation, on the hill for us there,
of a good leaf for a holy wafer.
Then the slim eloquent nightingale
from the corner of a grove nearby,
poetess of the valley, sings to the many
the Sanctus bell in lively whistling.
The sacrifice is raised
up to the sky above the bush,
devotion to God the Father,
the chalice of ecstasy and love.
The psalmody contents me;
it was bred of a birch-grove in the sweet woods

The contemporary Irish poet Dermot Bolger recalls how Christmas can evoke powerful memories (you may like to compare this with Tennyson's poem *In Memoriam*):

Absent Friends by **Dermot Bolger**

Dusk on Christmas Eve, a dozen tasks to be done.
The bustle of excited children playing downstairs,
Shopping that needs unpacking, decorations hung.

Amidst that bustle I sometimes find myself alone
In a bedroom, forgetting what I came up to fetch,
As I am swamped by a mosaic of faces once known.

Soon I will go down to celebrate with loved ones,
But I need to recall the shadows who shaped me first.
I open my bedroom window to let absent friends come.

The poetry of the Winifred Mustoe from Birmingham in England deserves to be better known. Here, she warns against those amongst us who are (in the words of the theatre director James Roose Evans) 'already dead':

Warning by **Winifred Mustoe**

If you meet with the dead, you must struggle to simulate death.
You must never betray
By a sentence, a glance, or a gesture, that pain or delight
Are only a sentence, a glance, or a gesture away.
Remember – the dead have no mercy, no insight, no fear,
But, scenting a wound, will disturb till they see the blood flow.
They will beat till the spirit is swollen and sore, and then go
With a snigger, a swagger, back into the silence of death.

If you meet with the dead, you must struggle to simulate death.
You must master the whole box of tricks –
The words that mean anything, nothing, the faces of stone,
The steps with the crowd, although never more deeply alone.
But the spirit within you – the suffering, quivering thing –
Let them never suspect. Let it suffer unseen and alone.
In the innermost deeps of your life let it suffer unseen –
And alone.

Plants – animals know this, and scientists call it
'Protective adaptation'.
If you meet with the dead – and you still wish to live, then remember –
Remember to simulate death.

Here is another poem that demonstrates how poetry can protest. It is
by the Canadian poet Lorne Crozier:

Without Hands by Lorne Crozier

(*In memory of Victor Jara, the Chilean musician whose hands were
smashed by the military to stop him from playing his guitar and singing
for his fellow prisoners in the Santiago stadium. Along with thousands
of others, he was tortured and finally killed there in September 1973.*)

All the machines in the world
stop. The textile machines, the paper machines,
the machines in the mines turning stones to fire.
Without hands to touch them, spoons, forks and knives
forget their names and uses, the baby is not bathed,
bread rises on the stove, overflows the bowl.
Without hands, the looms
stop. The music
     stops.

The plums turn sweet and sticky and gather flies.
Without hands
        without those beautiful conjunctions
those translators of skin, bone, hair
two eyes go blind
two pale hounds sniffing ahead and doubling back
to tell us
        of hot and cold or the silk of roses after rain
are lost
two terns feeling the air in every feather
are shot down.
Without hands my father doesn't plant potatoes
row on row, build a house for wrens,
or carry me
from the car to bed
when I pretend I'm sleeping.
On wash-days my mother doesn't hang clothes
on the line, she doesn't turn the pages of a book
and read out loud,
or teach me how to lace my shoes.

Without hands my small grandmother
doesn't pluck the chicken for our Sunday meal
or every evening, before she goes to sleep,
brush and brush her long white hair.

The Australian poet Judith Wright combines both narrative and lyric intensity in this short poem:

Blue Arab by **Judith Wright**

The small blue Arab stallion dances on the hill
like a glancing breaker, like a storm rearing in the sky.
In his prick-ears the wind, that wanderer and spy,
sings of the dunes of Arabia, lion-coloured still.

The small blue stallion poses like a centaur-god, netting the sun
in his sea-spray mane, forgetting
his stalwart mares for a phantom galloping unshod;
changing for a hear-mirage his tall and velvet hill.

This poem by the former British jet fighter pilot and poet Paddy Hughes, demonstrates how a local place can evoke universal concerns. Paddy regularly organises a festival of spoken poetry in London's Richmond Park and has created verse scripts for the video and TV programmes he makes:

Coffee Shop by **Paddy Hughes**

In Sheen
close by the spike
that annually prods us
with sombre reminders
of the dead and their deeds
there is a warm place.

It is a continental coffee place
rich with piquant meats and pies
and slices of doily-ed desserts.

It is a comfortable, friendly place,
a pavement oasis for slaking a thirst,
a first for informal business baguettes,
a natter-chit-chattering base
for artists and writers,
dust encrusted plasterers,
musty pensioners
and gangs of Mums
with prams.

It has a shop front window
lensed on the local world
and projects
a non-stop, widescreen film
of the passing cavalcade,
a criss-cross parade
of message-sided lorries,
shopping-laden ladies
and cars parking illegally.

It also had another set of windows
suspended on one side,
sun coloured vistas
of a cherished world ago,
sky blues, wheat creams,
sail whites, sea greens,
Balkan indigo,
orchards bursting with oranges,
grey men's squares with fountains,
fishing ports and mountains,
secret holiday haunts
before the civil war,
all frozen now
on the wall
in oils.

Dare
anyone
buy one
and steal
a vital part
of a prisoner's view.

And prisoners they are –
Madame and her charming family
serving at Montana –
prisoners of memory
and the terror
of Mostar.

But somehow,
a piece of the world away,
they soldier on
and smile.

In this next translation one of Israel's leading poets, Ra'hel speaks of
his love and concern for his country:

Our Garden by **Ra'hel**

Spring and early morning –
do you remember that spring, that day? –
our garden at the foot of Mount Carmel,
facing the blue of the bay?

You are standing under an olive,
and I, like a bird on a spray,
am perched on the silvery tree-top.
We are cutting black branches away.

From below your saw's rhythmic buzzing
reaches me in my tree,
and I rain down from above you
fragments of poetry.

Remember that morning, that gladness?
They were – and disappeared,
like the short spring of our country,
the short spring of our years.

Gwendolyn MacEwen was one of the most significant voices in recent Canadian poetry. In these next three poems she, like Wordsworth, Henry Normal and Gillian Bickley, reflects on relationships and on what poetry and poets can do:

Tall Tales by **Gwendolyn MacEwen**

It has been said that I sometimes lie, or bend the truth
    to suit me. Did I make that four hundred mile

    trip alone in Turkish territory or not?
    I wonder if it is anybody's business
    to know. Syria is still there,
    and the long lie that the war was.

Was there a poster of me offering money for my capture,
    and did I stand there staring at myself,
    daring anyone to know me? Consider
    truth and untruth, consider why they call them
    the theatres of war. All of us
    played our roles to the hilt.

Poets only play with words, you know; they, too,
    are masters of the Lie, the Grand Fiction.
    Poets and men like me who fight for something
    contained in words, but not words.

What if the whole show was a lie, and it bloody well was –
    would I still lie to you? Of course I would.

Animal Spirits by Gwendolyn MacEwen

Is it true, then, that one fears all that one loves?
These spirits are my awful companions; I can't tell
    anyone when they move in me.
They are so mighty they are unclear; it is the end
Of cleanliness; it is the great crime.

I can only kill them by becoming them. They are all
I have ever loved or wanted; their hooves and paws
    smell of honey and trodden flowers.

Those who do not know me sip their bitter coffee
    and mutter of war. They do not know
    I am wrestling with the spirits
    and have almost won. They do not know
I am looking out from the camels' eyes, out
    from the eyes of the horses.

It is vile to love them; I will not love them
                      Look –
my brain is sudden and silent as a wildcat.
                      Lord,
Teach me to be lean, and wise. Nothing matters,
nothing matters.

Late Song by **Gwendolyn MacEwen**

When it is all over – the crying and the dancing and the long
    exhausting music – I will remember only
How once you flirted with your death and lifted your dark
eyes
        to warn me of the world's end
As wild leaves fell, and midnight crashed upon the city.

But it is never over; nothing ends until we want it to.
    Look, in shattered midnights,
On black ice under silver trees, we are still dancing, dancing.

Meet me in an hour at the limits of the city.

Here is another piece from the contemporary British poet John Wright,
in which he rages against those who hold power over us:

Enigma Variation by **John Wright**

How come they, the compassionless, to power?
How come they, chilled and heartless, to the reins?
How come they, graceless spirits, to be leaders:
How come these undeserving by their gains?

They blunder, rhino-hided, all amongst us,
Insensitively trampling as they go,
Unwakened to the bruising of their passage,
Oblivious to the lovelessness they show.

Self-regarding, but forever downing others,
Lips chill strangers to the nourishment of praise;
Rule by fear – the only maxim they have trust in.
Confrontations feed the lusting of their days.

Will they come to know the seeping alienation
Consequent on misbegotten, heedless ways?
Will some unencumbered casualty-worker,
Truth telling, rip the filters from their gaze?

Or will they blunder on and on, unchallenged,
Delusion's victims; party to her sly deceit:
Believing, 'Oh how well we've managed!'
Nought to puncture the balloon of their conceit.

How come they, the compassionless, to power?
How come they, chilled and heartless, to the reins?
How come they, graceless spirits, to be leaders:
How come these undeserving by their gains?

Susan Hamlyn uses the classic lyric form, the sonnet, for her wry
comments on modern communications:

Interflora by **Susan Hamlyn** (STSD competition)

From Robert B@mailexcite.com
To Miss E B @virgin.uk
Please find herewith as proof of my esteem
a customised, fresh, virtual bouquet.
For scent please click on cellophane and press
Control. To read the message on the tag
highlight the print, click on Encrypt Reverse.
To unwrap blooms and place in vase use Drag.
My flowers sent, beloved, in this way,
won't fade, stink of mortality's decay.
Petals won't wilt to husks nor leaves to slime;
These on-line flowers for you will outlast time.
But if, my love, this gift seems incomplete
and does touch your heart, then press Delete.

The following poem demonstrates how an encounter with poetry can still take us by surprise. It was read to me as a member of a group visiting one of England's lesser-known stately homes: Grimsthorpe Castle. As we approached the house from a deep valley our guide read this poem to us, recently written by Andrew Hawes, to evoke the experience of centuries of visitors. 'Vauday' means 'God's Valley' and refers to a location where a monastery had been demolished and the stone was used to build the castle. The poem has been set to music by the poet's brother, the distinguished composer Patrick Hawes:

Carriageway by **Andrew Hawes**

Horsechestnut candles light the carriageway,
which from the highest point the park surveys –
the distant house, then dips behind the trees,
and sweeps through open farmland green with wheat.

The wooden bridge with white rails Vauday keeps
separate, secret – where ancient memory sleeps.
The steep – wooded valley nave-like arches high,
In dappled – green cool shade the cattle lie.

Then out into the open park it runs
past shining water drowned in morning sun,
and high above, the House all stately stands
and crowns the oak-dressed pasture land.

The journey made through park and wooded grange
pass by a thousand years of chance and change.
The carriageway in classic splendour ends;
proving the certain permanence of men.

We conclude this entire collection of pieces with a poem from Winifred Mustoe that highlights the pleasure of perusing an anthology:

Surprise by **Winifred Mustoe**

It seemed to appear from nowhere – that cluster of foxgloves
Under a hedge bordering a busy street,
Pealing a silent carillon of beauty
Over the drab grey scene,
Sharing a tiny space with some trailing ivy
And bits of litter between.

I thought of anthologies
Where a poet little known, perhaps unknown –
But read with delight – might scatter a small winged seed
Into some crevice of a stranger's mind,
Into a stranger's need.

To root and grow and flower
Briefly, or, maybe, through a long winter
Of lost direction, a landscape dark with fear;
So that the spirit, trudging abroad, and weary,
Might glimpse some colour breaking through frozen places
And gather the brightness there.

SOURCES

Every effort has been made to trace copyright owners, but where that has not been possible the editor will gladly rectify this in future editions.

Birmingham and Midland Institute, Margaret Street, Birmingham, B3 3BS for poems by Winifred Mustoe.

The poems *Exit, Survival* and *Welcome* were first published in, Gillian Bickley, *For the Record and other Poems of Hong Kong, Proverse Hong Kong* (ISBN 962855702-5) supported by the Hong Kong Arts Development Council. Distributor: Chinese University Press, Shatin, Hong Kong.

Dramatic Lines Publishers, PO Box 201, Twickenham, TW2 5RQ for *What is the Matter with Mary Jane, Advent Journey, Introducing Oscar, Feminine Zones and Hard Boiled.*

Methuen Ltd, 11 New Fetter Lane, London, EC4P 4EE for *The Mahabharata.*

Anthea Preston, 68a Mickleburgh Hill, Herne Bay, CT6 6DX for *Vita and Harold* and *Monday Nights Have Got to be Better.*

Pat Whittock, Forge Cottage, High Street, Sharnbrook, Bedfordshire, MK44 1PF for poems by Trevor Whittock.

John Wright, Westbourne House, Lower Street, Eastry, CT13 OJG for *Enigma Variations* and *Short Term Tenants..*

The Editor, Hilltop Publishing, PO Box 429, Aylesbury, Bucks, HP18 9XY for *The Wind in the Pylons.*

Susannah Pickering-Saqqa, 131 Brookscroft Road, Walthamstow, E17 4JP for *Joha and the Ten Donkeys*.

John Murray (Publishers), 338 Euston Road, London, NW1 3BH for extracts from *A Time of Gifts*.

Michael Frohnsdorff, The Marlowe Society, 75 Alexander Drive, Faversham, ME13 7TA for synopsis and information on *Lust's Dominion*.

Triple D Books: zdenholm@tripledbooks.com.au for poems by Colin Thiele, Anne Bell, Bill Scott and Max Fatchen.

The Editor, *Speech and Drama*: Fampell@aol.com for winning poems in the STSD competition.

Caravan of Dreams: Synergetic Press, 24 Old Gloucester Street, London, WC1 for *Gilgamesh* and *Marouf the Cobbler*.

New Island Books, 2 Brookside, Dundrum Road, Dublin 14 Ireland for *Desert Lullaby* in *Contemporary Irish Monologues*.

Bryan Harnetiaux and David Casteal, 517 East 17th Avenue, Spokane, WA 99203, USA for *York*

J. Garnet Miller Ltd, 10 Station Road, Colwall, Worcestershire, WR14 6RN for: *The Midlands Mysteries, Troilus and Criseyde* and *The Smuggler's Leap* taken from *The Ingoldsby Legends*.

Poetry for Palestine C/O Agnes Meadows: Agnesmorgn@aol.com for *The Back Step*.

The Rev. Andrew Hawes, The Vicarage, Edenham, Bourne, PE10 0LS for *Carriageway*.

Lewis Allan for *The Kiss*.

Sheffield Popular Publishing, Aizlewood's Mill, Nursery Street, Sheffield, S3 8GG for the poems of Henry Normal.

Penguin Books, Harmondsworth, Middlesex for Charles Perrault's *Fairy Tales, Manon Lescaut* and the prose version of *Gilgamesh.*

Mrs Kamala Ramchandri-Naharwar: kamala333@vsnl.net for *The Big 'A'* and *The Panchatandra.*

Dr Geraldine Trevella: geraldine.trevella@cranford.pegasus.net.nz for the poem by Charlotte Trevella.

Bantam World Classics for the *Promenade* taken from *The New Underground Theatre* and for *Miss Julie* taken from *Strindberg: Seven Plays.*

Signet Classics for *School for Wives* taken from *Tartuffe and Other Plays by Moliere.*

Wave Crest Classics, 12 Wave Crest, Whitstable, Kent, CT5 1EH for *Medea.*

John Ward: www.johnward.org.uk for *The Iron Bridge.*

Details of all other extracts and translations may be found in the text or by contacting the Editor: kennethpickering@talktalk.net

For Your Own Poems